Praise for *Dual Momentum Investing*

This is an excellent book on the various forms of price momentum: why they work, including a very clever way to use them. I highly recommend investors read this book.

—James P. O'Shaughnessy, author, *What Works on Wall Street*;
Chairman and CEO, O'Shaughnessy Asset Management

Gary Antonacci takes us on a comprehensive tour of investment methods, exploring their strengths and weaknesses, and lays out a strong case for combining absolute and relative momentum. I consider *Dual Momentum Investing* an essential reference for system designers, money managers, and investors.

—Ed Seykota

I was familiar with Antonacci's writing talent when he won first place in the 2012 NAAIM Wagner Paper contest, which I chair. *Dual Momentum Investing* is a treasure of well-researched momentum-driven investing processes. After a thorough and enlightening review of historical momentum writings and a brief, critical review of modern portfolio theory, he clearly shows a number of different methods that anyone who is serious about a long-term strategy will find easy to implement. This is one of those five-star books; it is logical and easy to grasp.

—Gregory L. Morris, Chief Technical Analyst
and Investment Committee Chairman,
Stadion Money Management, LLC; author, *Investing with the Trend*

In *Dual Momentum Investing*, Gary Antonacci presents a clear and scholarly sound case for the success of a simple momentum-based strategy. It is easy to implement, yet its quantitative nature helps you avoid your own behavioral biases. Give it a try; you'll be hooked!

—John Nofsinger, PhD, Seward Chair of Finance,
University of Alaska Anchorage; author, *The Psychology of Investing*

Gary Antonacci's *Dual Momentum Investing* is what happens when "Ed Thorpe's *Beat the Dealer* meets Seth Klarman's *Margin of Safety*." *Dual Momentum* presents a thoughtful and tantalizing "do what you know and know what you're doing" investment process. This is an ambitious and must-have book.

—Claude Erb, retired Managing Director, TCW Group, Inc.

This is a must-read for both individual investors as well as financial advisors. It will forever change the way you think about developing investment and asset allocation strategies.

—Dr. Bob Froehlich, retired Vice Chairman, Deutsche Asset Management

Gary Antonacci provides a fantastic and valuable viewpoint of dual momentum investing. This book is highly informative, substantive, and readable for the sophisticated investor. Gary presents a well-crafted balance between academic findings and application of this emerging topic.

—Victor Ricciardi, Coeditor, *Investor Behavior:*
The Psychology of Financial Planning and Investing

Few authors can review the breadth of competing investment theories and practices in such an accessible manner. Even fewer can make their own contributions. Gary Antonacci's *Dual Momentum Investing* achieves both.

—Jerry Waldron, PhD, former Assistant Professor
of Finance, University of Memphis
and Assistant Professor of Management, New York University
Stern School of Business

Gary Antonacci's book *Dual Momentum Investing* opens up a secret world—the power of momentum investing—that has been hidden in plain sight for decades.

—Kurt Brouwer, Chairman, Brouwer & Janachowski, LLC

DUAL MOMENTUM INVESTING

DUAL MOMENTUM INVESTING

AN INNOVATIVE STRATEGY FOR HIGHER RETURNS WITH LOWER RISK

GARY ANTONACCI

New York   Chicago   San Francisco   Athens   London
Madrid   Mexico City   Milan   New Delhi
Singapore   Sydney   Toronto

7 8 9 10   LCR   21 20 19 18 17

ISBN   978-0-07-184944-9
MHID   0-07-184944-0

e-ISBN   978-0-07-184945-6
e-MHID   0-07-184945-9

This publication is designed to provide accurate and authoritative information in regard to the subject matter covered. It is sold with the understanding that neither the author nor the publisher is engaged in rendering legal, accounting, securities trading, or other professional service. If legal advice or other expert assistance is required, the services of a competent professional person should be sought.

> —*From a Declaration of Principles Jointly Adopted by a Committee of the American Bar Association and a Committee of Publishers and Associations*

Library of Congress Cataloging-in-Publication Data
Antonacci, Gary.
  Dual momentum investing : an innovative strategy for higher returns with lower risk / by Gary Antonacci.
    pages cm
  Includes bibliographical references and index.
  ISBN-13: 978-0-07-184944-9 (alk. paper)
  ISBN-10: 0-07-184944-0 (alk. paper)
  1. Investments. 2. Investment analysis. I. Title.
  HG4521.A6197 2015
  332.6—dc23
                                                                2014022568

McGraw-Hill Education books are available at special quantity discounts to use as premiums and sales promotions or for use in corporate training programs. To contact a representative, please visit the Contact Us pages at www.mhprofessional.com.

Contents

FOREWORD

EUGENE FAMA, THE 2014 CORECIPIENT of the Nobel Prize in Economics and father of the efficient market hypothesis, has three words to describe momentum: "momentum is pervasive." This is no small admission from Dr. Fama. Yet, despite momentum being pervasive, it remains largely, and perhaps curiously, misunderstood by investors. Thankfully, we have Gary Antonacci to fill this void. Gary's *Dual Momentum Investing* is a true "pracademic" masterpiece, bridging the gap between academics, who have explored the nuanced theoretical mechanics of the momentum anomaly in dense academic journals, and practitioners who have used their vague knowledge of momentum in an ad-hoc way to generate excess returns. Gary brings to bear his expertise in both spheres, creating a momentum-based asset allocation strategy that is robust, simple, implementable, and has historically earned an outsized risk-adjusted return.

You could be forgiven for being skeptical, as I once was, about the merits of Gary's Dual Momentum Investment philosophy. After all, there are many second-rate or even wholly ineffectual efforts to capture momentum. And as any empirical researcher can tell you, "trust, but verify." Notwithstanding our extensive and rigorous examination, the evidence clearly suggests that Gary's simple, intuitive, and comprehensive model is worth the effort it takes to understand it.

One of my best friends, who happens to be a former market maker for the largest emerging debt players in the world and who, not coincidentally, has already retired to Miami at the ripe old age of 40, often tells me, "Rising prices attract buyers; falling prices attract sellers." In as many words, my friend is describing the momentum effect. Gary takes the momentum phenomenon—that every trader intuitively understands and uses—to a higher level, and one that is accessible to investors of all stripes.

Why did it take so long for a book like *Dual Momentum Investing* to hit the market? The answer is straightforward: it took a unique author, and there is only one Gary. He is a singular figure in the world of momentum. My relationship with Gary was born via the same mechanism through which I meet many fascinating folks: a blog romance. I was thinking about a momentum-related content piece for TurnkeyAnalyst.com, a blog dedicated to democratizing quantitative investing, and Gary's paper "Absolute Momentum: A Simple Rule-Based Strategy and Universal Trend-Following Overlay" came across my desk. I immediately thought, "This won't do. Here we go again—another practitioner posing as a serious academic researcher." But then I read Gary's paper. The further I read, the more impressed I became. The paper was well written, clear, scientific in its construction, and read like an academic journal article. I couldn't understand why the author wasn't employed at a university. I had to learn more.

After multiple conversations via e-mail and phone, I decided I had to meet Gary in person. Consistent with how these blog romances evolve, we scheduled a "geek date" at the 2013 Western Finance Association Annual Meeting in Lake Tahoe. As I waited in the lobby of the Hyatt Regency watching herds of famous (and infamous) academics scurry along to the various sessions, a curly haired, low-profile man confidently strolled through the fancy double doors in a pair of jeans and a short-sleeved collared shirt. This was no tweed-clad academic with Coke bottle glasses. I pointed in his direction and asked, "Gary, is that you?" Gary responded with a wide smile, "Wes? Hey man, let's hurry up and catch the session on inferring arbitrage capital from return correlations!" And so it was that our curious blog relationship began to blossom into a full romance.

We were running late, so we ran out the door toward the lake where the finance sessions were under way. We arrived, sweaty and winded—probably not in a condition to open the door on an ongoing paper presentation and get the death stare from 50+ finance professors. I suggested, "Gary, let's just chill out, grab some coffee, and we can hit the next paper presentations."

Little did I know, I was about to get a presentation far superior to anything that was going on behind the many closed doors.

Gary and I strolled outside with our coffee, and he started shedding some light on his background. "So there I was, in the Army and on my way to combat as a medic . . ." I interrupted, "Wait, you are a Vietnam vet? I was a captain in the United States Marine Corps and an Iraq vet!" We both looked at each other, amused at this unanticipated congruity. I knew that a military background often drives certain character traits that are useful in the investing world. Next, Gary continued describing his unique background, "Yeah, I've done some cool things. I lived in India for a few years, went on tour as a comedy magician for a while, was an award-winning artist, and I have an MBA from the Harvard Business School." Perplexed, I had to stop him, "Say again?"

After about an hour went by and my head stopped spinning from listening to the various exploits Gary had engaged in over the years, I had to ask him the question: "Gary, sounds like you're a guy that never wanted to get a real job—why didn't you become an academic? You'd be perfect!" And of course, as I should have anticipated, he replied, "Wes, funny you ask. I almost followed your same path when I was your age. I applied to the Chicago Finance PhD program and was accepted. I really wanted to be an academic researcher." It all began to make sense. I questioned, "Well, what happened?" Gary, always ready with the right answer, replied, "Well, I almost pursued that opportunity, but I was making a ton of money trading options. Plus, I didn't believe in the efficient market hypothesis, and I worried that if I entered the program I would have to give up making money because they were saying the markets couldn't be beat!" I pondered Gary's response and thought that had I been faced with the same opportunity, I would probably have done the same thing.

So what is the moral of the story here, and why have I spent so much time describing my relationship and experience with Gary? My hope is that you can identify, as I did, that Gary is a unique person with unique talents. Gary has a way of compiling massive amounts of research from diverse areas and synthesizing it in such a way that even a struggling momentum half-wit like me can actually comprehend what is going on. And make no mistake.

What Gary has done is extremely challenging. It requires broad-ranging knowledge and an ability to connect the dots across many domains. I know, because I have tried. My own research on value investing and behavioral finance led to my coauthored book on value investing, *Quantitative Value*. My takeaways were similar to Gary's. My book serves as a reminder that (1) I will never be Buffett, and (2) combining a systematic decision process with a sound investment philosophy has historically been a successful way to compound wealth over time. Gary's book also provided some reminders: (1) I will never be able to write as clearly as Gary, and (2) momentum investing is a top-shelf anomaly, similar to, if not better than, the value anomaly. I was feeling a bit jealous.

I'm excited to find out what people think of Gary's great book about momentum investing. Unlike the value-investing space, where investment offices are plastered with "classics," there really isn't a classic text on momentum investing. In Gary's work, we may have an instant classic. I think Gary's *Dual Momentum Investing* should be the first book on everyone's momentum shelf. I hope everyone enjoys the read as much as I did, and most importantly, I hope you learn something that makes you a better investor in the future.

Wesley R. Gray, PhD
Executive Managing Member, Empiritrage
Coauthor of *Quantitative Value*

ACKNOWLEDGMENTS

If I have seen further, it is by standing on the shoulders of giants.

—*Isaac Newton*

I NEVER COULD HAVE WRITTEN THIS book had it not been for the substantial body of work by so many dedicated momentum researchers over the past 80 years. I am particularly indebted to Alfred Cowles III and Herbert E. Jones, who painstakingly hand-calculated and published the very first quantitative study of momentum in 1937. Practitioners today, me included, still incorporate momentum in much the same way that Cowles and Jones presented it.

I wish to thank Wes Gray for his encouragement in getting me to put words to paper. Wes and his associate, David Foulke, also gave me valuable feedback on this book's content.

I am indebted to Tony Cooper for his insightful comments and worthwhile contributions to this book. I also appreciate the useful suggestions that Cheryl Becwar, Riccardo Ronco, Charles W. ("Bill") White, and John Hardin gave me. Finally, I am grateful to my excellent editorial team of Jonathan Lobatto, Dr. Stephen Miller, Larry Pell, and Kyra Kitts for their kind and helpful assistance.

PREFACE

Profit in the share market is goblin treasure; at one moment, it is carbuncles, the next it is coal; one moment diamonds, and the next pebbles. Sometimes they are the tears that Aurora leaves on the sweet morning's grass; at other times, they are just tears.
　　　　　　　　　　　—*José de la Vega*, Confusion of Confusions, *1688*

A CCORDING TO THE RESPECTED MIT financial economist Andrew Lo (2012), "Buy and hold doesn't work anymore. The volatility is too significant. Almost any asset can suddenly become much more risky."[1] Even Warren Buffett's Berkshire Hathaway, Inc. lost nearly 50% of its market value on two separate occasions since 1998.

Mohamed El-Erian, former head of PIMCO, said, "Diversification alone is no longer sufficient to temper risk. You need something more to manage risk well." Diversification has long been called the only free lunch in investing. Now somebody needs to pay for that lunch. Because financial markets have become progressively more integrated and correlated, multiasset diversification can no longer protect investors from severe market losses. Such losses can cause investors to overreact and convert temporary setbacks into permanent ones by closing out their investments prematurely.

What we need now is a new paradigm that dynamically adjusts to market risk and keeps us safe from the vagaries of today's highly volatile markets. We need a way to earn long-term above-market returns while limiting our downside exposure. This book shows how momentum investing can make that desirable outcome a reality.

Momentum, or persistence in performance, has been one of the most heavily researched finance topics over the past 20 years. Academic research has shown momentum to be a valid strategy from the early 1800s up to the present, and across nearly all asset classes. After many years of such intense scrutiny, the academic community now accepts momentum as the "premier anomaly" for achieving consistently high risk-adjusted returns.[2]

Yet momentum is still largely undiscovered by most mainstream investors. I wrote this book to help bridge the gap between the academic research on momentum, which is extensive, and its real-world application, which is still minimal.

The first goal of this book is to explain momentum principles so readers can easily understand and readily appreciate them. I present the history of momentum investing and bring readers up to speed on modern financial theory and the possible reasons why momentum works. I then look at a wide range of asset choices and alternative investment approaches. I finally show how dual momentum—a combination of relative strength and trend-following methods that I introduced in two award-winning research papers—is the ideal way to invest.

I develop and present an easy-to-understand, straightforward application of dual momentum that I call Global Equities Momentum (GEM). Using only a U.S. stock market index, an all world non-U.S. stock market index, and an aggregate bond index, I show how investors using GEM could have achieved long-run returns nearly twice as high as the world stock market over the past 40 years while avoiding severe bear market losses.

I am always amazed when I think of how much time and effort most people put into accumulating wealth and how little study and effort they put into finding the best ways of preserving and growing that wealth. Warren Buffett says that risk comes from not knowing what you are doing. This book should help remedy that situation and steer you in the right direction.

Dual Momentum Investing is more than just an introduction to momentum investing ideas. It is also a practical guide to help investors and investment professionals tune in with market forces and profit from this newfound knowledge.

I have tried to make the book interesting and useful to as many readers as possible. I include some advanced material for those interested in an in-depth treatment of the subject, while also keeping the book understandable to more casual readers. I provide a glossary for those who may need help with the vocabulary of modern finance. So, let us get started.

DUAL
MOMENTUM
INVESTING

CHAPTER 1

WORLD'S FIRST INDEX FUND

Never trust the experts.

—*John F. Kennedy*

I NDEX FUNDS ARE WELL KNOWN today. Many think John McQuown and Bill Fouse at Wells Fargo (which became Barclays Global Investors) started the first index fund in 1971 when they invested in every New York Stock Exchange (NYSE) stock for the Samsonite pension fund. However, that is not correct. Let me tell you how it really happened.[1]

I discovered the real first index fund during a chance meeting I had while working at Smith Barney & Co. in 1976. At that time Smith Barney was a prestigious investment banking and institutional brokerage firm similar to Goldman Sachs, Salomon Brothers, and First Boston. Along with the rest of the Street at that time, Smith Barney wanted more of a retail distribution network, so they had recently acquired Harris Upham, a retail-oriented wirehouse. As is usual after these kinds of acquisitions, Smith Barney let go the redundant operations of Harris Upham. However, Harris Upham had one of the best over-the-counter (OTC) departments in the business, headed up by Bob Topol, who was in charge of all their OTC activity.

In those days, there was no electronic marketplace. In order to buy or sell OTC securities, one had to phone around to different brokerage firms and check the bid/offer spreads maintained by each of their market makers. A top-notch OTC market maker could become a terrific profit center for a firm. This was not only because the bid/offer spreads of OTC securities were sometimes large enough to drive a small vehicle through them. The best OTC market makers also profited from their acumen in maintaining large inventories of OTC stocks. They could slant their bids and offers to end up with larger positions in stocks they really liked, and smaller or short positions in those they disliked. Bob was one of the very best stock pickers in the business. Top institutional investors would deal with him in order to find out his view of the stocks they were interested in, as well as to be able to execute their trades in the large, liquid inventories that Bob routinely maintained.

Smith Barney was proud to have Bob onboard. They sent him around to all their offices so representatives could learn more about Bob and feel comfortable directing business his way. Soon after the merger, Bob came around to our office to introduce himself and explain what he could do for us. It was not Bob and what Bob did that opened my eyes, but rather it was the story that he told us.

Bob arrived about an hour before lunch and gave an impressive presentation explaining some of the finer points of OTC market making. It was obvious to everyone there why Bob was so admired and respected. One of my colleagues complimented Bob on his superior trading ability and his profit-generating capability. Bob thanked him, sat back in his chair, paused a moment, then casually remarked, "Yes, I've done well, but would you like to hear about someone who has done better than me? In fact, this person has done better in the market than anyone else I know."

We all quickly sat back down. Bob had our complete attention. As we stared at him inquiringly, Bob continued, "The best investor I know—one who has outperformed all the professional money managers I'm familiar with—is my wife, Dee. Would you like to hear how she does it?"

Sasquatch could have walked into the room, and no one would have noticed. Here was Bob, one of the industry's top traders and market makers, who did business with some of the world's best money managers, telling us that his wife did better at investing than all of them! Now he was about to tell us how she did it. As they say, you could have heard a pin drop.

Ignoring our stunned silence, Bob continued, "Dee has always been very patriotic. So years ago she decided to buy all the stocks with 'U.S.' or 'American' in their names. She bought U.S. Steel, U.S. Shoe, U.S.

Gypsum, U.S. Silica, American Airlines, American Brands, American Can, American Cyanamid, American Electric Power, American Express, American Greetings, American Home Products, American Hospital Supply, American International Group, American Locomotive (this was a while ago), American Motors, American South African, American Telephone & Telegraph, British American Tobacco, North American Aviation, Pan American Airlines . . . and many smaller companies."

Some of us started smiling. We did not know if Bob was serious or if he was putting us on. However, Bob seemed sincere and continued, "Dee did very well this way. After a number of years, she wanted to buy some additional stocks. Since she admired General Eisenhower and General MacArthur, she decided to buy all the Generals: General Dynamics, General Electric, General Mills, General Motors, General Maritime, General Steel, General Telephone, Dollar General, Mercury General, Media General, Portland General Electric. . . . Since then, Dee has continued to do better with her portfolio than anyone I know, and that's the God's honest truth."

Everyone smiled at Bob and seemed amused as we adjourned for lunch. However, for days, and then weeks, I could not stop thinking about Dee. Dee had access to some astute investment information herself. Not only had she been married to Bob for almost 30 years, but Dee's father had owned an OTC market-making firm. I kept asking myself how Dee could have out-performed the world's best money managers for so long with such a naïve strategy. Had she just been incredibly lucky? After a few weeks, the answers came to me.

WHY IT WORKED

First, Dee's portfolio had relatively little in the way of transaction costs. She bought stocks only once and held onto them forever. Commissions were a lot higher back then, and this was a significant cost saving. In addition, Dee's permanent portfolio was not subject to ill-timed buy and sell decisions based on emotional responses to market performance. We will see later that this is often a significant drag on investor returns.

Lack of portfolio turnover and emotionally based decision making were not the whole story, however. Dee also did not have to pay management fees to anyone. That saved her at least 1% per year, compared to what investors paid who were in mutual funds or other managed investment programs.

Finally, Dee's portfolio was well diversified. This was not true of most investor portfolios at the time. They usually had a bias toward a particular investment style, such as defensive, growth, large cap, and so on. Back then, large-cap "glamour" stocks, such as Avon, Coke, Disney, IBM, Kodak, McDonald's, Merck, Polaroid, and Xerox, were very popular. These "Nifty-Fifty" sometimes sold at enormous price/earnings (P/E) ratios. For example, in the 1970s, McDonald's' P/E was 68, Johnson & Johnson's was 62, and Coca-Cola's was 48. Extreme P/E ratios like these could be justified only if those companies had growth rates such that the value of, say, Avon stock would now exceed the gross domestic product (GDP) of some countries. The noted economist Kenneth Boulding once said, "Anyone who thinks steady growth can continue indefinitely is either a madman or an economist."[2]

Dee's randomly constructed portfolio did not have a particular bias or investment style. It was like the market itself—equally balanced among small cap, large cap, value, growth, and just about every other factor. In fact, Dee's portfolio was a more balanced portfolio than the Standard & Poor's 500 Index, with its large cap and growth stock tilt. Dee had unwittingly created the world's first index fund, and a good one at that. She did so without the need for brokers, money managers, or anything else, except a dictionary.

LESSONS LEARNED

The reasons for Dee's success were a life-changing revelation for me. Here are the lessons I took away from my understanding of why Dee was successful:

- It is important to keep costs as low as possible. This is the easiest way to earn risk-adjusted excess return (alpha).

- One should diversify broadly, and not just by picking stocks with different names having similar characteristics. One should diversify with respect to company size, investment style, industry concentration, and other biases.

- It is not easy to beat the market. Very few investors do. Replicating the market portfolio may be a good thing.

Based on these realizations, I decided to quit the brokerage business. It no longer made sense for me to be a stock jockey saddling investors with high costs and overconcentrated portfolios trying to beat similar accounts handled by other stock jockeys to an ever-elusive finish line.

I saw there were now two options left for me with respect to professional investment management. The first was to become an efficient marketeer, which sounded similar to being a Mickey Mouseketeer and, to me, was no less silly. I viewed efficient markets like I viewed Ptolemaic astronomy, with both based largely on a priori assumptions. My second option, according to those in academic finance at that time, was to become like Don Quixote, tilting at the windmills of efficient market theory.

EFFICIENT MARKETS

By the mid-1970s, the efficient market hypothesis (EMH) had made a strong impression on the minds of otherwise sensible people. EMH is the belief that prices of stocks fully reflect all publicly available information about them. This means that no one can expect to beat the market consistently.

I had toyed briefly with the EMH idea. I applied and was accepted into the finance PhD program at the University of Chicago, which was the bastion of EMH. However, I never attended due to frightening thoughts I had of being tarred and feathered as a heretic on the University of Chicago quadrangle.

The idea behind efficient markets actually got its start in the 1800s when Charles Dow (founder of Dow Jones & Co. and the *Wall Street Journal*) commented on the market as an efficient processor of information: "In fact, the market reduces to a bloodless verdict all knowledge bearing on finance, both domestic and foreign. The price movements, therefore, represent everything everybody knows, hopes, believes, and anticipates." In his 1889 book called *The Stock Markets of London, Paris, and New York*, George Gibson wrote, "Shares become publicly known in an open market. The value which they acquire may be regarded as the judgment of the best intelligence concerning them." Followers of EMH later claimed as their own the concept that prices reflect all available public information.

A more substantive rationale for EMH appeared in the PhD thesis of Louis Bachelier in 1900. Bachelier compared the behavior of stock market buyers and sellers to the random movement of particles suspended in fluid. Bachelier concluded that stock price movements are random, and it is impossible to make predictions about them. Prior to this, in 1863, Jules Regnault used a randomness model to say that the deviation of stock prices is directly proportional to the square root of time. Bachelier, however, was the first to accurately model stochastic processes. These were called Brownian motion, after the Scottish botanist Robert Brown, who in 1826 first noted the random movements of pollen grains suspended in water. Einstein got the credit for explaining Brownian motion mathematically in 1905, but Bachelier had already done so in his PhD dissertation written five years earlier. Bachelier was also way ahead of his time with respect to his pioneering work on probability theory.[3]

Bachelier turned his PhD thesis into a book published in 1900 called *The Theory of Speculation*. It did not attract much attention until the statistician Leonard "Jimmy" Savage rediscovered it while doing research on the history of probability. Savage was so impressed with Bachelier's pioneering work with respect to speculative markets that he sent postcards about it to a dozen or so economists he knew in the mid-1950s.

Paul Samuelson had been working on similar ideas himself. He was delighted to hear from Savage and find out about Bachelier. It allowed Samuelson to put all the pieces together into a unified equilibrium framework based on Bachelier's work. In 1965, Samuelson published a seminal paper using Bachelier's ideas about efficient markets and Samuelson's own proof to support it.

Samuelson went on to write the bestselling economics textbook of all time in which he strongly endorsed EMH. Samuelson was the first American to receive the Nobel Prize in Economic Sciences. This was in 1970, the second year of the award.

Although I had looked into EMH, I had also read most of the practical books I could find on investing, such as those by Graham and Dodd (1951),

Darvas (1960), Thorp and Kassouf (1967), and Levy (1968). (I will describe the work of Darvas and Levy, who used relative strength momentum-based investing, in more detail in the next chapter.)

I was also familiar with some well-respected mutual fund managers, such as John Neff, William Ruane, Walter Schloss, and Max Heine, and I had an exceptional hedge fund manager as a client. All had consistently outperformed Mr. Market. I could not believe that outperformance by such astute investors was due only to chance or luck. The outcomes of these investors seemed clearly at odds with what academics were saying. While academics were extolling the virtues of EMH, practitioners like these were doing something completely different, and they were succeeding.

Andrew Lo, one of the first economists to look thoroughly at market pricing anomalies, tells how years ago he did some rigorous research on technical analysis. He identified predictable patterns in stock prices, which, to academics back then, was akin to voodoo. Lo presented his encouraging results to an MIT colleague who responded, "Your data must be wrong."[4]

According to the "joint hypothesis," one can only say if a market is or is not efficient with reference to a model of equilibrium returns. If such a model can predict the market, then either the model is wrong or markets are not efficient. Lo must have done some very good research for his colleague to think up a third alternative, that of erroneous data. In the words of Nietzsche, "convictions are more dangerous enemies of truth than lies." EMH had become a belief system with many firm adherents, not unlike religion. George Soros (2003), the world's most successful hedge fund manager, who has earned $39.6 billion in net gains, called EMH "market fundamentalism." Hallelujah! Throughout the 1970s and 1980s EMH ruled supreme.

Warren Buffett wrote in his 1988 Berkshire Hathaway chairman's letter, "Amazingly, EMH was embraced not only by academics, but also by many investment professionals and corporate managers as well. Observing correctly that the market was *frequently* efficient, they went on to conclude that it was *always* efficient. The difference between these propositions is night and day."[5]

Other indications also pointed away from perfectly efficient markets and investor rationality. These included premiums on closed-end fund and government-backed mortgage securities that are not arbitraged away, and ubiquitous market bubbles that imply substantial deviations of prices from intrinsic values over extended periods.

ALTERNATIVES TO PASSIVE INVESTING

Even though I knew that the market was very hard to beat, I came to believe that it was not impossible to do so. For better or worse, I took upon myself the formidable task of trying to identify and exploit true market anomalies and inefficiencies. Don Quixote, move over.

In the late 1970s, I had the idea, long before Long-Term Capital Management (LTCM), of managing a derivatives-based hedge fund. There were no publicly available data feeds back then, so I hired an electrical engineer to tear apart a quote machine, dump the data into a microprocessor, and then feed that into our office minicomputer. I formed partnerships with market makers on all the option exchange floors, did well initially, and then suffered the same fate as later befell LTCM. This was due to the same reasons of overleverage coupled with highly unusual events. I, however, did not reach the "limits of arbitrage" and require the intervention of the Federal Reserve to keep from destroying the world's financial system.[6] I tried to learn from that experience and move on, still convinced that there were anomalies out there ready to be exploited.

In the early 1980s, I had another promising idea and started commodities pools that used my own Bayesian-based portfolio optimization model to allocate capital to some of the world's top traders, such as Paul Tudor Jones, Louis Bacon, Richard Dennis, John W. Henry, Al Weiss, Tom Baldwin, and Jim Simons. These traders not only were very successful; their results were also largely uncorrelated to one another due to their different trading approaches and diverse portfolios. Portfolio optimization fit this situation to a tee, and my investment partnerships prospered.

As I watched Paul Tudor Jones trade for us, I came to know beyond any doubt that I had been correct in rejecting EMH. I felt fully vindicated in venturing outside the realm of efficient market theory. I did not know, however, if I would ever again find another opportunity that was this rewarding.

However, I was motivated to keep looking. Commodity trading has capacity constraints. Some of the best traders end up returning investor funds and trading mostly their own accounts, which is what happened with several of my traders. In addition, the generous commodities risk premium that speculators enjoyed from the 1970s to the 1990s had largely dissipated by the 2000s. Speculator participation had risen sharply, and there were many more speculators around to share in the limited amount of risk premium provided by hedgers. It was time to move on. Little did I know at the time that it would take nearly 20 years before I would find another opportunity to exploit market trends using what is essentially the same principle—systematic price momentum.

THE TIDE STARTS TO TURN

By the 1990s, behavioral finance had become popular. With it came challenges to rational expectations and the EMH. The Nobel laureate Robert Shiller (1992) wrote, "This argument for the efficient market hypothesis represents one of the most remarkable errors in the history of economic thought. It is remarkable in the immediacy of its logical error and in the sweep and implications of its conclusions."

Before then, prominent economists sometimes had to hide in the active management closet. Charlie Munger, Warren Buffett's right-hand man, wrote, "One of the greatest economists of the world is a substantial shareholder in Berkshire Hathaway and has been for a long time. His textbook taught that the stock market was perfectly efficient, and that nobody could beat it. But his own money went into Berkshire Hathaway and made him wealthy."[7]

According to *Fortune* magazine, that economist was the same Paul Samuelson whose bestselling textbook championed the cause of efficient markets and who had published an academic proof in support of EMH![8]

Samuelson's 1974 paper, "Challenge to Judgment," is what inspired John Bogle of Vanguard to start the first public index fund in 1976. Afterward, Samuelson wrote the following about what some referred to as Bogle's folly, "I rank this Bogle's invention along with the invention of the wheel, the alphabet, Gutenberg printing, and wine and cheese; a mutual fund that never made Bogle rich but elevated the long-term returns of the mutual-fund owners. Something new under the sun."[9]

So here we have Samuelson inspiring the first public index fund and then praising it to the high heavens, while Warren Buffett actively manages Samuelson's own money. Maybe the wheel, the alphabet, and Gutenberg printing were not that great after all.

THE MOMENTUM ANOMALY

As more people began questioning EMH orthodoxy, an intriguing area started appearing in the academic literature. The burgeoning field of behavioral finance led some to question whether investors always acted rationally and in their own best interests. People acting in emotional and irrational ways could cause prices to depart systematically from their fundamental values in predictable ways. Maybe the markets could be beat after all, since irrational investors might allow anomalies to persist. In light of this possibility, momentum started to receive attention from the academic community beginning in the early 1990s. Behavioral factors could be used to explain many of the characteristics of momentum.

After years of momentum research by many academics, even Eugene Fama and Kenneth French, two of the founders of EMH, began paying attention to momentum, which they called the "premier anomaly."[10] Momentum was powerful, persistent, and not explainable by any of the commonly known risk factors.

Not only did momentum research benefit from EMH losing its hold over modern finance, but the findings of momentum researchers added considerably to the body of knowledge that itself contradicted the efficient markets hypothesis.

The following chapters will show how I combined the best elements of academic momentum research, added a few ideas of my own, and came up with a simple and practical method for generating exceptional profits with less risk by using momentum. Furthermore, I will show how you can apply this methodology to the largest liquid markets having high expected long-run returns.

Before doing this, I will introduce you to the history of momentum theory so you can understand and appreciate momentum's historical effectiveness and longevity. I will also show how momentum fits into the strange and mysterious world of modern finance. Then we will look at the logical underpinnings behind momentum to help you better understand how and why it works. Next, we will look at asset choices and alternative investment opportunities. I will then be ready to present a simple and effective momentum-based model that you can use.

After presenting my model, I will explore other momentum approaches and additional applications using dual momentum. By the end of the book, you should have a good understanding of momentum, as well as everything you need to know in order to reap its rewards.

CHAPTER 2

WHAT GOES UP . . . STAYS UP

It may be that the race is not always to the swift, nor the battle to the strong, but that's the way to bet.

—Damon Runyon

S O WHAT IS MOMENTUM? IT is the tendency of investments to persist in their performance. Investments that have done well will continue to do well, while those that have done poorly will continue to do poorly.

CLASSICAL IDEAS

Momentum investing has a long and distinguished history. I will take you through its evolution. The idea of momentum began with Newton's first law of motion: every object in a state of uniform motion tends to remain in that state of motion. It is unlikely Sir Isaac had investing in mind when he came up with this law. If he did, then he should have paid more attention to apples falling from trees and reminded himself that what goes up, must come back down. Newton lost a fortune in the South Seas stock bubble of 1718–1721 by buying too late and holding on too long. Newton afterward said, "I can calculate the movement of stars, but not the madness of men." Alas, poor Newton was not alone in that regard.

The first notable person to express momentum principles in investment terms was the great classical economist, David Ricardo. Ricardo wisely considered downside as well as upside momentum when he said in 1838, "Cut your losses; let your profits run on." Ricardo followed his own advice and retired at the age of 42, having amassed a fortune of $65 million in today's dollars.

MOMENTUM IN THE EARLY
TWENTIETH CENTURY

Momentum principles in the form of a disciplined investing style were alive and well early in the twentieth century. Momentum dominates much of the famous book *Reminiscences of a Stock Operator* by journalist Edwin Lefèvre (2010), originally written in 1923. It describes the thoughts and exploits of legendary trader Jesse Livermore. Livermore once said, "Big money is not in the individual fluctuations, but in sizing up the entire market and its trend." Trend following is a form of momentum investing. Livermore introduced the momentum idea of buying stocks when they are making new highs. His statement "Prices are never too high to begin buying or too low to begin selling" accurately describes momentum style investing.

Richard Wyckoff also wrote books beginning in the 1920s that drew heavily on momentum principles. In his 1924 book, *How I Trade in Stocks and Bonds: Being Some Methods Evolved and Adapted During My Thirty-Three Years Experience in Wall Street*, Wyckoff advocated buying the strongest stocks within the strongest sectors and within the strongest index when they were trending up during the marking up phase of their accumulation-distribution cycle. Wyckoff used his ideas to amass a fortune in the stock market before he retired to a 9.5-acre estate and mansion in the Hamptons, next to Alfred P. Sloan, the legendary chairman of General Motors.

In his bestseller, *The Seven Pillars of Stock Market Success*, George Seamans (1939) recommended that traders buy stronger stocks during an advance and short weaker stocks during declines, which is very much in tune with relative strength momentum investing.

On the quantitative side of things, beginning in the late 1920s, Arnold Bernhard, founder of the Value Line Investment Survey, successfully used relative strength price momentum in conjunction with earnings growth momentum. According to the Value Line website, Group 1 stocks are those ranked highest in performance over the past year and that had accelerating earnings growth. From 1965 through 2012, Group 1 stocks had an average annual gain of 12.9% before dividends, while the S&P 500 gained 6.1%. Group 5 stocks had a –9.8% annual loss. Dividing a stock's latest 10-week average relative performance by its 52-week average relative price is the price momentum factor still used today by Value Line.

H. M. Gartley developed momentum-based relative velocity ratings in the 1920s. The Dow theorist Robert Rhea (1932) subsequently published these ratings in his book *The Dow Theory*. Gartley (1945) himself wrote an article titled "Relative Velocity Statistics: Their Application in Portfolio Analysis" for the *Financial Analysts Journal*. In that article Gartley wrote, "In addition to the usual valuation methods applied to stock, analysts should consider its velocity. The velocity statistic is a technical factor in the stock's price volatility that measures the percentage rise and fall of a stock against an average." This was yet another way to express relative strength price momentum.

In his 1935 book *Profits in the Stock Market*, Gartley introduced the world to trend-following moving averages. Bernhardt and Gartley were both early pioneers of quantitative, rules-based momentum strategies.

The first truly scientific study and published academic paper on momentum was by Alfred Cowles III and Herbert E. Jones (1937). Cowles was a prominent economist who founded the Cowles Foundation for Economic Research, initially at the University of Chicago and now at Yale. There were no computers back then, so Cowles and Jones painstakingly hand-compiled stock performance statistics from 1920 through 1935. This was a remarkable accomplishment at that time. Cowles and Jones found that the strongest stocks during the preceding year had a very strong tendency to remain strong during the following year. In their own words, "Taking one year as the unit of measurement for the period 1920 to 1935, the tendency is very pronounced for stocks which have exceeded the median in one year to exceed it also in the year following." The same basis underlies today's relative strength momentum approach to investing, and the conclusions of Cowles and Jones are just as valid today as when they were first revealed in 1937.

MOMENTUM IN THE MID-TWENTIETH CENTURY

In the 1950s, George Chestnutt published a newsletter that ranked relative strength momentum of both stocks and industries. Here is some advice Chestnutt gave his newsletter readers:

> Which is the best policy? To buy a strong stock that is leading the advance, or to shop around for a sleeper or behind-the-market stock in the hope that it will catch up? On the basis of statistics covering thousands of individual examples, the answer is very clear as to where the best probabilities lie. Many more times than not, it is better to buy the leaders and leave the laggards alone. In the market, as in many other phases of life, the strong get stronger, and the weak get weaker.

Chestnutt (1961) also wrote a book on relative strength investing and used this approach to manage successfully the American Investors Fund. From January 1958 through March 1964, this fund had a cumulative return of 160.5%, versus 82.6% for the Dow Jones Industrial Average.

Chestnutt never became well known, but another momentum investor and mutual fund manager at the time did. He was Jack Dreyfus, also known as the Lion of Wall Street.

Dreyfus began his career using a $20,000 loan, and he retired a billionaire. Here is how he described his investment philosophy: "If you've got an escalator that's going up, you're better off betting on an individual on that escalator than on an individual on an escalator that's going down." Dreyfus bought stocks only when they broke to new highs off sound chart patterns. His Dreyfus Fund was up 604% from 1953 to 1964, compared to 346% for the Dow Jones Industrial Average.

Two small funds at Fidelity started to emulate Dreyfus's investment technique. They were managed by Edward "Ned" Johnson II, the founder of Fidelity Management & Research in 1946, and Gerald Tsai, manager of the Fidelity Capital Fund. Tsai, a colorful figure, championed momentum and increased the popularity of momentum investing to the point that he became the first mutual fund manager to gain celebrity treatment in the press. He founded the Manhattan Fund in 1965, expecting to raise $25 million in the fund's first year. Instead, Tsai attracted $275 million during the fund's first day.

Dreyfus also influenced William O'Neil, publisher of *Investor's Business Daily*. O'Neil's motto was "buy the strong, sell the weak." One of the key features of O'Neil's well-known CAN SLIM method was to buy stocks that outperformed other stocks and sell those that underperformed. This idea is right out the momentum playbook. O'Neil said, "What seems too high in price and risky to the majority goes higher eventually, and what seems low and cheap usually goes lower." [1] O'Neil's book *How to Make Money in Stocks*, featuring his CAN SLIM approach, has sold over two million copies since 1988.

Also in the 1960s, Nicolas Darvas (1960) wrote several inspiring and entertaining books, including the popular *How I Made $2,000,000 in the Stock Market*. The book describes his adventures as a professional dancer traveling the world while sending off buy and sell cables to his broker. Darvas would buy strong stocks making new highs, hold them until their momentum began to wane, and then replace them with new price leaders.

Gilbert Haller (1965) advocated a similar "strongest stocks" strategy in his book, *The Haller Theory of Stock Market Trends*. George Soros (2003) used a variation of momentum that he called positive feedback "reflexivity" in order to accumulate large profits with conglomerates and real estate investment trusts (REITs) in the 1960s and 1970s. According to Soros, buying begets further buying in a self-reinforcing process. We will see in Chapter 4 that positive feedback trading due to behavioral factors is one of the key characteristics of momentum.

Momentum has always been the engine behind speculative commodity trading. Richard Donchian launched the first managed futures fund in 1949. Donchian thought price movements in stocks and commodities were often too optimistic or pessimistic because they reflected the emotions of the people trading them. He believed that trend followers could profit from this overextension of prices.

In 1960, Donchian began a weekly commodities newsletter that featured his 5- and 20-day moving average trend-following system. His well-known 4-week channel breakout method inspired other great traders like Ed Seykota and Richard Dennis. Dennis taught his Turtle Traders a version of Donchian's channel breakout system, and a number of them went on to become very successful commodity trading advisors.[2] Seykota also trained a number of highly successful traders, such as Michael Marcus and David Druz, and developed the first large-scale commercial computerized trading system. Jack Schwager said about Seykota in his first *Market Wizards* book, "the accounts Seykota managed have witnessed an absolutely astounding rate of return. . . . I know of no other trader who has his track record over the same length of time."[3] Seykota later launched "Ed's Six Step Program" to help other trend traders.[4]

During the 1970s and 1980s, the torch of momentum investing passed to successful hedge fund managers who were often reticent to talk about their activities. One prominent momentum investor, however, was the outspoken philanthropist and mutual fund manager, Richard Driehaus.

Driehaus began his investment career in 1968. He manages over $10 billion following a momentum strategy similar to the ones used by Darvas, Chestnutt, and Haller—rotational, relative strength investing using top-performing stocks. In 1970, *Barron's* named Driehaus to its "All Century" team of 25 persons who have been the most influential within the mutual fund industry over the past 100 years. Jack Schwager (2008) featured Driehaus in his book *The New Market Wizards*, as did Peter Tanous (1999) in his book *Investment Gurus*. Here are a few quotes from Driehaus describing his momentum-based approach:

> Perhaps the best-known investment paradigm is buy low, sell high. I believe that more money can be made by buying high and selling at even higher prices. . . . I try to buy stocks that have already had good price moves, that are already making new highs, and that have positive relative strength. . . . I always look for the best potential performance at the current time. Even if I think that a stock I hold will go higher, if I believe another stock will do significantly better in the interim, I will switch.

Even before serious academic research on momentum began in earnest in the 1990s, it was hard to dismiss the practical value and impressive results of relative strength momentum investing.

MODERN MOMENTUM

The first computer-based study of momentum was by Robert A. Levy (1967). Levy coined the phrase "relative strength," which is a good way to characterize this style of investing. Academics later renamed this systematic, quantitative approach "momentum," which is a more generic term also used by practitioners to mean buying strong stocks. Discretionary dot-com traders ("gunslingers" who thought a horse is easiest to ride in the direction it is already going) during the 1990s were often called momentum players. This confusion between systematic, rules-based momentum and seat-of-the-pants discretionary momentum persists even today. Levy's term "relative strength" is a much more accurate description of quantitative, rules-based momentum, but Levy presented his findings before momentum became respectable to the academic community. When academics caught on to momentum, they probably did not want to have their work associated with Levy. They preferred instead to engage in identity theft by changing the name from *relative strength* to *momentum*. They were either unaware that this term *momentum* was already being used by practitioners to mean something similar but different—or they just did not care.

Levy's initial study covered five years of data using 625 NYSE stocks. Levy (1968) later expanded his study and wrote a book on the subject of relative strength investing. Levy said:

> The stocks which historically were among the 10% strongest appreciated in price by an average of 9.6% over a 26-week future period. On the other hand, the stocks which historically were among the 10% weakest appreciated in price an average of only 2.9% over a 26-week future period.

Michael Jensen, a respected academic, criticized Levy for ignoring transaction costs and risk factors.

Later, Akemann and Keller (1977) demonstrated superior relative strength results after transaction costs when using S&P industry groups from 1967 through 1975. Bohan (1981) showed attractive results applying relative strength momentum to 11 years of S&P industry group data. Brush and Boles (1983) presented evidence of excess returns from relative strength momentum applied to 18 years of stock data, even after adjusting for transaction costs and risk. Despite the growing evidence of abnormal profits from momentum investing, even after accounting for costs and risk factors, there was still little interest in momentum among academics.

During this time, belief among academic researchers in efficient markets was still prevalent, which is a major reason why momentum never got the attention or respect that it deserved. Many academics still thought stock market returns followed a random walk process, similar to Brownian motion, where aggressive competition among market participants to exploit any predictable patterns made price changes random and unpredictable. As the saying goes, if your only tool is a hammer, everything looks like a nail. Academics pounded on momentum until it was barely noticeable.

This began to change in the 1980s. Nobel laureate Robert Shiller (1981) published "Do Stock Prices Move Too Much to Be Justified by Subsequent Changes in Dividends?" This paper showed that historically stocks were more volatile than would be expected if investors were strictly rational. Keim and Stambaugh (1986) presented evidence that stock returns contain predictable components. In 1987, evidence that stock prices could seriously deviate from their fair values got a boost when the stock market fell over 20% in a single day. This one-day collapse strained the limits of rationality. Academics had also begun documenting persistence in stock prices due to positive serial correlation, which contradicts the random walk theory of stock price movement.[5] De Bondt and Thaler (1985) had identified a long-term reversal effect in stocks whereby investors correct excessive overvaluation or undervaluation. These all cast doubts on perfect market efficiency.

Behavioral finance also started gaining traction as a way of explaining the growing number of market anomalies, such as price momentum and mean reversion. The academic community had begun to wake up and take notice. Behavioral finance is the study of the influence of psychology on the behavior of investors and the effect this has on markets. Behavioral biases helped to resolve some of the growing disconnect between theory and reality in the world of finance. Chapter 4 will shed more light on the rational and behavioral aspects of momentum, including how they help explain why momentum works and why it is likely to continue to work in the years ahead.

SEMINAL MOMENTUM RESEARCH

With behavioral finance now as a way to explain momentum logically, momentum research took a giant leap forward with the publication of "Returns to Buying Winners and Selling Losers: Implications for Stock Market Efficiency" by Jegadeesh and Titman (1993). They found, using data from 1965 through 1989, that winning stocks on the NYSE and American Stock Exchange (AMEX) over the past 6 to 12 months continued to outperform losing stocks on average over the next 6 to 12 months by approximately 1% per month after adjusting for any return differences due to other risk factors. This outperformance was essentially the same thing that Cowles and Jones had discovered 30 years earlier. Eight years after their 1993 paper, Jegadeesh and Titman (2001) followed up with an out-of-sample validation of their work and found that 1990–1998 past winners outperformed past losers by approximately the same 1% per month. This, and considerable subsequent momentum research on additional data by others, did away with concerns that momentum profits could be attributable to data mining biases.

Quantitative research helped to transform momentum from a discretionary approach to a rules-based one. Jegadeesh and Titman's research clearly showed that stocks strongest over a 3- to 12-month look-back (or formation) period are also the strongest ones over comparable future periods. This was especially true with respect to a 6- to 12-month look-back window.

According to rules-based momentum, you buy the strongest 10% to 30% stocks over the past 6 to 12 months, hold them 1 to 3 months, then reevaluate and rebalance the portfolio. As an added bonus, a rules-based approach such as this helps remove behavioral bias from the decision-making process and lessens the chance that investors will make poor decisions based on emotional responses to market conditions.

ADDITIONAL MOMENTUM RESEARCH

The rigorous and replicable research done by Jegadeesh and Titman inspired a great many additional momentum research papers. In fact, momentum has become one of the most heavily researched finance topics over the past 20 years. Since Jegadeesh and Titman, there have been more than

300 academic papers on momentum, including over 150 in the last five years. Research has focused on four areas:

- Determining the momentum effect across different assets

- The statistical properties of momentum returns

- Theoretical explanations for the momentum effect

- Enhancements to momentum-based strategies

Continuing research has established momentum as an anomaly that works well within and across nearly all markets, including U.S. and foreign equities, industry groups, equity indexes, global government bonds, corporate bonds, commodities, currencies, and residential real estate.[6] Momentum works well across over a dozen asset classes and more than 40 countries.[7]

Momentum is robust with respect to time, as well to different markets. Chabot, Ghysels, and Jagannathan (2009) showed that momentum worked well in U.K. equities all the way back to the Victorian age. Geczy and Samonov (2012) showed that momentum was effective through out-of-sample testing on U.S. equities all the way back to the year 1801! Over this 212-year history the equally weighted top one-third of stocks sorted on price momentum significantly outperformed the bottom one-third of stocks by 0.4% per month with a highly significant t-statistic of 5.7.

In the 1990s, Schwert (1993) did a study of market anomalies related to profit opportunities, such as value, size, calendar effects, and momentum. He found that all anomalies except momentum disappeared, reversed, or attenuated following their discovery. Momentum was the only one that persisted.

Momentum has continued to perform well out-of-sample during the two decades following the seminal studies by Jegadeesh and Titman. It is no wonder that Fama and French (2008) call momentum "the center stage anomaly of recent years." They further explain:

> The premier market anomaly is momentum. Stocks with low returns
> over the past year tend to have low returns for the next few months,
> and stocks with high past returns tend to have high future returns.[8]

Readers can easily satisfy themselves as to the efficacy of momentum by reviewing some of the important academic research papers referenced in this book. You can download many of them from the Social Science Research Network (SSRN) website or by doing an Internet search on their titles or authors' names.[9] You can also find additional information on my website and associated blog: http://optimalmomentum.com.

CURRENT APPLIED MOMENTUM

Dorsey, Wright & Associates (DWA) introduced the first publicly available systematic momentum-based program in 2007. DWA manages two mutual funds and four broad-based exchange-traded funds using a proprietary approach that selects 100 (200 for small cap) individual stocks using relative strength momentum. Its broad-based funds cover U.S. large-cap/mid-cap, U.S. small-cap, developed market, and emerging market stocks. DWA reassesses and rebalances its momentum-based portfolios quarterly.

In 2009, AQR Capital Management (AQR) established three momentum-based mutual funds covering U.S. large-cap/mid-cap, U.S. small-cap, and international stocks. AQR's funds select the top one-third of stocks using momentum measured over a 12-month look-back period, excluding the last month. AQR usually rebalances positions quarterly. In Chapter 9, I show how AQR's U.S. large-cap/mid-cap relative momentum index has performed since its inception.

BlackRock's iShares is the latest firm to offer a popular, publicly available momentum product. In 2013, iShares introduced an exchange-traded fund (ETF) based on the Morgan Stanley Capital International (MSCI) USA Momentum Index that holds 100 to 150 stocks using a combination of 6- and 12-month look-back periods. The fund weights its positions based on volatility and rebalances them semiannually.

All of these publicly available products apply relative strength momentum to individual stocks. They therefore miss the potential risk-reducing benefits of cross-asset diversification. Using momentum with individual stocks also results in substantially higher transaction costs than applying momentum to broad asset classes and indexes. AQR, for example, estimates transaction costs of its U.S. momentum index to be 70 basis points per year.

Also important is the fact that while relative strength momentum can enhance returns, it does little to reduce volatility or maximum drawdown. These risks may even increase compared to similar portfolios using nonmomentum, buy-and-hold strategies.

In Chapter 7, we will discuss absolute momentum, which can enhance expected returns like relative momentum does. However, unlike relative momentum, absolute momentum can also reduce extreme downside exposure that is associated with long-only investing. Absolute momentum aims to beat the market by avoiding the beatings. In Chapter 8, we will construct a simple and practical investment model using dual momentum, which is the amalgamation of both relative and absolute momentum.

CHAPTER 3

MODERN PORTFOLIO THEORY PRINCIPLES AND PRACTICES

> A physicist, a chemist, and an economist are stranded on an island
> with nothing to eat. A can of soup washes ashore. The physicist
> says, "Let's smash the can open with a rock." The chemist says,
> "Let's build a fire and heat the can first." The economist says,
> "Let's assume we have a can opener. . . . "
>
> —*George Goodwin ("Adam Smith")*

IN THIS CHAPTER,* I GIVE an overview of modern finance and its relationship to dual momentum.[1] I also show why we should sometimes
be skeptical of the "experts." In the words of the well-regarded economist
Joan Robinson, "The purpose of studying economics is not to acquire a set
of ready-made answers to economic questions, but to learn to avoid being
deceived by economists." We will see in later chapters how a healthy dose
of skepticism toward those with initials behind their names might keep
us from being sold a bill of goods for investments we may not really need
or want.

---

* This and the next chapter are a bit wonkish. Some readers may wish to skip them and move
  on to Chapter 5.

MARKOWITZ MEAN-VARIANCE OPTIMIZATION

In 1952, a young economics student at the University of Chicago, Harry Markowitz, developed an ingenious way to construct efficient portfolios, which he defined as those offering the highest expected return at any given level of risk (volatility), or, conversely, the lowest amount of risk at any specified level of expected return. Markowitz had taken an idea out of the realm of operations research (quadratic programming) to create an optimization algorithm that he used to map out the "frontier" of these efficient portfolios. Prior to this, there had been no quantitative way of simultaneously using expected return, volatility, and correlation to determine optimal portfolio combinations. Markowitz called his methodology mean-variance optimization (MVO).

During the oral exam defending his Ph.D. thesis, Markowitz was challenged by Milton Friedman for over an hour. Friedman argued that Markowitz's research was not economics, business administration, or even mathematics. Markowitz received his PhD anyway and went on to become the father of modern portfolio theory. He received the Nobel Prize in Economic Sciences mainly for his PhD thesis work.

On the practical side of things, there are problems, however, in implementing MVO. As is common with many economic models, the assumptions underlying MVO do not fit the real world very well.[2] MVO results are unstable when the covariance (the combination of correlation and volatility) matrix is ill conditioned, which is brought about by having very similar assets. MVO results are also highly sensitive to the inputs used. These can give unreliable results, since MVO maximizes the estimation errors of these inputs. Small input differences can lead to large output differences. This has led to MVO creating error maximizing portfolios.

Users of MVO often have to adjust the inputs, constrain them to reduce sampling error, or incorporate prior information to shrink the estimates back to values that are more reasonable. Return inputs are particularly unreliable, and some MVO users ignore them entirely by opting to use instead a minimum variance portfolio. DeMiguel, Garlappi, and Uppal (2009) showed that any gains from optimal diversification were more than offset by estimation errors. MVO produces extreme weights that fluctuate substantially over time and performs poorly out of sample.[3] Equal portfolio weighting is usually superior to MVO as a practical matter.[4] While MVO theory was elegant and impressive, like many other modern financial models, it did not hold up well in the real world. However, researchers did not realize this during the early years of MVO.

What they did realize is that computers had limited power back in the 1950s, and MVO was computationally demanding. MVO could require matrix inversions involving covariances and returns of thousands of assets. A 1,000-asset portfolio, for example, would require 550,000 covariances.

Therefore, in the early to mid-1960s, a number of academic researchers working independently developed a simplified alternative to MVO called the capital asset pricing model (CAPM).[5]

CAPITAL ASSET PRICING MODEL

What early CAPM did was a linear regression between the excess return (return less the risk-free rate) of an asset (or portfolio of assets) and the excess return of the market index. A linear regression determines the relationship between two or more variables and provides measures that allow you to determine the accuracy of that relationship.

The beta coefficient of the CAPM regression equation tells you the sensitivity of an asset's excess return to variations in the market's excess return. In other words, it tells you how much the market's movement contributes to your return. CAPM also tells you that the expected return on any security is proportional to the risk of that security as measured by its beta.

The intercept of the regression equation is the alpha. It is what you have left over once you remove beta from the equation. Alpha represents abnormal profits. It is what you earn in excess of the reward for assuming market risk.

Instead of having to deal with possibly thousands of inputs to construct optimal portfolios, with CAPM you only need information pertaining to your portfolio of stocks and the market index. If you diversify among a number of stocks spread out in different industries, you could target the expected return and volatility you want for your portfolio by targeting the average beta of your stocks. Equally important from an academic point of view, you could use CAPM to help determine a firm's cost of capital and to measure investment performance on a risk-adjusted basis. An annual alpha of 1% means your risk-adjusted excess return is 1% a year. Using CAPM, you could judge investment management skill just by tracking a portfolio's alpha. Economists also liked the fact that statistical significance could be associated with alpha and beta in the form of t-statistics and probability values.

They say there are two ways to gain a positive expected return. The first is by taking on known risk factors (beta). The second is by outsmarting everyone else (alpha).

There was just one problem with CAPM; it did not work very well in empirical testing. Returns of high beta portfolios were too low, and returns from low beta portfolios were too high. Much of the variation in expected return was unrelated to a portfolio's beta.

In the early 1980s, I came across an academic paper that tried to explain commodity returns in terms of single-factor CAPM. This paper was actually used in a graduate-level finance class at Berkeley. I wondered at the time, "What does the stock market have to do with the price of tea in China, or the price of any other commodity?" I was also aware at the time of the statistical problems associated with CAPM. Financial market returns, in general, violate the standard linear regression assumptions of drawing from distributions that are independent and identically distributed.[6]

CAPM ignored too many risks. Mark Twain reportedly said, "It ain't what we don't know that gets us in trouble. It's what we know for sure that just ain't so." Fischer Black said, "In the end, a theory is accepted not because it is confirmed by conventional empirical tests, but because researchers persuade one another that the theory is correct and relevant."

By the 1990s, academics had more evidence that all was not well with CAPM. Future returns on low P/E, low book-to-market, and small-cap stocks appeared to be higher than predicted by their betas. This resulted in the seminal Fama and French (1992) study that expanded CAPM from a single factor to a three-factor model by adding value and size risk factors to the single market factor. This well-known study suggested that the book-to-market ratio and market capitalization could explain the cross-sectional variation in average equity returns better than just the market factor alone. So now, we had three factors instead of just one. Not long afterward, Carhart (1997) added a fourth factor representing cross-sectional momentum.

Academics then became factor happy. At least 82 of them have been published in leading academic journals. Searching diligently for explanatory factors is reminiscent of Procrustes, the Greek mythological figure who made his visitors fit his bed by either stretching them or cutting off their legs.

Data snooping biases can arise from focusing on anomalous data. Harvey, Liu, and Zhu (2014), after applying to a variety of market risk factors a significance deflation adjustment for data mining bias, concluded, ". . . many of the factors discovered in the field of finance are likely false discoveries. . . . Echoing a recent disturbing conclusion in the medical literature, we argue that most claimed research findings in financial economics are likely false."[7]

CAPM was just not that reliable. For followers of CAPM, the real world was an annoying special case. Empirical tests showed that high beta and high volatility stocks did not give the return advantage that they should, according to three- or four-factor CAPM. Fama and French (2004) stepped forward and called CAPM "empirically vacuous." They noted "whether the model's problems reflect weakness in the theory or in its empirical implementation, the failure of the CAPM in empirical tests implies that most applications of the model are invalid."

CAPM not only had empirical problems. It, along with other models of modern finance, also had theoretical issues. Financial models generally rely on two main assumptions. The first is that market prices adhere to a normal or lognormal distribution.[8] The second assumption of modern finance is that prices are independent of one another. Yesterday's prices should have no influence on today's prices.

Mandelbrot (2004) courageously challenged both these assumptions. He demonstrated that market prices do not follow a normal distribution, but rather one associated with unstable variance and fatter tails denoting a higher frequency of extreme events. Mandelbrot identified this as a Cauchy distribution. Others have called it a stable Paretian, Pareto-Levy, or Levy-Mandelbrot distribution. Whatever you call it, this distribution means that catastrophic drops in stock prices can happen more frequently than a normal distribution would suggest.

As for independence, Mandelbrot made a case that even if prices are not autocorrelated, their volatility is correlated over time. This means that big price swings tend to cluster, and it is likely that stocks will move by an above-average amount, even if we do not know the direction of the move. According to Mandelbrot, because the two main assumptions of modern finance are flawed, related models such as CAPM are also flawed. They understate market risk and the amount of capital financial institutions should hold to withstand market risk.

Unfortunately, many academics stopped paying attention to Mandelbrot's financial concepts once they realized that these concepts challenged the usual assumption suspects, which had become part and parcel of most financial models. Mandelbrot's unbounded, nonfinite variance calculations were also difficult to work with.[9]

Despite their many empirical and theoretical challenges, linear factor models do give some indication of the relationship between risk and expected return. Researchers still routinely use linear three- and four-factor models to measure the performance and statistical significance of investment strategies. Factor models may have some value as a general guide to the strength and significance of a strategy. Therefore, we will use them in Chapter 8 as one way to confirm the results of our momentum model.

Warren Buffett, who rivals Yogi Berra as originator of some of the world's best quotes, once said, "Beware of geeks bearing formulas." In terms of developing models that can accurately explain and deal with the real world, financial economists have not been very successful. Researchers have tried to come up with a number of fixes along the way, such as resampling adjustments for MVO and a complicated array of additional factors for CAPM. Effective results are still questionable, at best. In the words of Robert Haugen (2010):

> We can advance by developing radically new theories to help us understand what we now see in the data. Or we can go back, denying what is now readily apparent to most, bending the data through ever more convoluted processes until it screams its compliance with our preconceptions.

BLACK-SCHOLES OPTION PRICING

Other financial models may give us additional insight into the workings of modern finance. Option-pricing theory began in 1900 when Bachelier saw how options could control risk and tried to figure out how to price them. Bachelier reasoned that if an option was a "fair bet," then it had to have a fair value. He was not entirely successful in computing fair option values, but he was not far off either. Subsequent efforts to price options were complex or awkward, and they often depended on individual risk preferences.

Since the time of Irving Fisher, economists have been enamored with the tidiness of equilibrium-based models. Inspired by Bachelier's random walk ideas, Thorp and Kassouf (1967) came up with an equilibrium-based options model, but their published work did not discount back the expected value of an option at expiration.

It was Fischer Black and Myron Scholes who published the first complete equilibrium-based option-pricing model. It resulted in Nobel prizes, since the economic community loves equilibrium-based models. The Black-Scholes option-pricing model (the BS model) became a favorite and a showpiece among financial economists.

Option-pricing models can be useful in helping users transfer risk by using derivatives. Investors were quick to recognize this. In 1970, there was almost no trading in financial derivatives. By 2004, outstanding derivative contracts totaled $273 trillion.

Besides increasing the popularity of derivatives, pricing models also gave some users a false sense of security. As we will see in Chapter 4, we tend to overweight our own skills and knowledge, which causes us to suffer from an illusion of control and underestimate the odds of bad events and unfavorable outcomes.

In addition to the near meltdown of the world's financial system in 1998 due to the Long-Term Capital Management (LTCM) debacle, derivatives contributed to the bankruptcy of Orange County, California, the collapse of Barings Bank, and, of course, the global financial crisis of 2007–2008. Warren Buffett referred to derivatives as "financial weapons of mass destruction."

Institutional investors were slow to learn their lessons. Following the collapse of LTCM in 1998, Merrill Lynch warned that mathematical risk models "may provide a greater sense of security than warranted; therefore, reliance on these models should be limited."[10] No one listened to them at that time.

However, we shouldn't blame only the tools and not the workers who use them. One can make a case that these financial crises were due in large part to institutions using derivative models without exercising proper judgment or fully understanding their true risks. Derivative buyers of convoluted mortgage obligations should have listened to Nobel laureate George Akerlof who said, "If you are in a market and someone is trying to sell you something which you don't understand, you should think they are selling you a lemon."

The BS model had one interesting feature compared with other financial models. When people said, "Hey, finance isn't rocket science," financial economists could now answer, "Oh yes, it is!" Robert Merton (a Nobel laureate with a background in engineering mathematics) added Ito's lemma to the BS model. Rocket scientists use Ito calculus to track the trajectory of rockets by breaking up the notion of continuous time into infinitely small pieces until it becomes a continuum. Not only did BS make economics look more like a science, it made it look like rocket science. Noble laureate Paul Krugman's statement about economists could easily apply to financial economists: "As I see it, the economics profession went astray because economists as a group mistook beauty, clad in impressive looking mathematics, for truth." In the words of Robert Heilbroner, "Mathematics has given economics rigor, but alas, also mortis."[11]

The biggest problem with the BS model is its inaccuracy when dealing with extreme price movement. The lognormal distribution of prices that underlies the BS model can underestimate the probability of risky events by a factor of 10.

Practitioners long ago replaced the BS model with a more realistic binomial pricing model, yet academics still count the BS model as one of the great discoveries of modern finance. In the words of Nobel laureate Robert Shiller, "Economics is usually some kind of story that we tell that we think approximates reality, but we can get carried away with our stories."

PORTFOLIO INSURANCE—NOT!

Another hailed innovation of modern finance was portfolio insurance. This concept was developed by several finance professors who said investors should increase their long exposure when markets move up quickly and decrease their long exposure when markets drop quickly. This is supposed to create an effect similar to derivatives hedging. However, anyone with much practical experience could sense this might not be a good idea, since markets are short-term mean reverting. More often than not, they overreact to information, then reverse.

The public often reacts incorrectly by selling into weakness and buying into strength. Portfolio insurance does the same thing. For those who remember when they were the main sources of short-term market liquidity and price stabilization, stock exchange specialists and floor traders made a good living doing the opposite of portfolio insurers while trading against the public.

October 19, 1987, was the single worst day in stock market history. The S&P 500 dropped by 22% that day and by over one-third in a day and a half. Portfolio insurance reinforced that selling pressure. The 1988 Presidential Task Force on Market Mechanism, also known as the Brady Report, concluded that one-third of the selling that day was related to portfolio insurance. Portfolio insurance helped turn a market correction into a full-scale panic. Portfolio insurers packed up their bags following this market collapse and subsequent rebound ("mean reversion happens") that gave them large whipsaw losses.

It also did not help advance the cause of efficient markets that prices could reflect values 20% lower than they had been just one day earlier. It was hard to say over both those days that the "Price Is Right."

Belief in self-adjusting, rational markets may bear some responsibility for the global financial crisis of 2007–2008. As Paul Volcker said, "It's clear that among the causes of the recent financial crises was an unjustified faith in rational explanations and market efficiencies." Others have blamed the efficient market hypothesis for indifference to "irrational exuberance" and chronic underestimation of the dangers of asset bubbles breaking. Perhaps Volcker made some sense when after the last financial crisis he said that the only worthwhile financial innovation of the past 20 years was the automated teller machine.

BETTER LIVING THROUGH FINANCE

To be fair, there have been some useful things that have come from the world of finance over the past 75 years. First was the idea that to reduce substantially the company-specific risks inherent in holding equities, one should construct portfolios of at least 25 to 30 diverse stocks. Getting rid of diversifiable risk this way is as close as one can get to a free lunch with respect to investing. This realization helped spur the popularity of mutual funds and other pooled investment vehicles. According to the Investment Company Institute, there were only 170 mutual funds in 1965 with $35 billion in assets. By 2012, there were 7,596 funds with over $13 trillion in assets.[12]

The second important finding of modern finance was greater awareness of the high price that investors pay for professional investment management. Much of the time, benefits do not justify the costs involved. Modern finance theory and empirical testing led directly to the development of index funds, which have been of great benefit to those who have been receptive to them.

The third important development in modern finance came from the field of psychology. Behavioral finance can explain many of the inconsistencies we see between financial theory and practice. It can also help investors better understand their unrewarded psychological tendencies and serve as a guideline for more enlightened behavior.

The fourth beneficial finding of modern finance is momentum as first presented in a systematic way by Cowles and Jones in 1937. Since then, researchers have validated its usefulness in hundreds of subsequent studies. While academics remained busy engineering more complex ways to model financial markets, simple momentum has stood the test of time as the premier market anomaly.

CHAPTER 4

RATIONAL AND NOT-SO-RATIONAL EXPLANATIONS OF MOMENTUM

A theory is more impressive the greater the simplicity of its premises, the more different kinds of things it relates, and the more extended its range of applicability.

—*Albert Einstein*

I F YOU ASK MOST ACADEMICS about the effectiveness of momentum, they will likely say that it works very well. If you ask them why it works so well, you may get a blank stare. To say we really do not know why momentum works would make this a very short chapter. So instead, I will give a number of possible reasons that *may* explain why momentum works, even though the underlying answer is still that we do not exactly know.

There are several reasons why it may be a good idea to try to understand why and how momentum works. First, knowing this may give us more confidence in using momentum.

Next, knowing how and why momentum works could give some insight into how the markets in general function. This may be useful in helping us understand the psychological biases that affect investor behavior in general, as well as our own behavior and motivations as investors.

Third, understanding the basis underlying momentum can help us develop models that can better exploit the momentum anomaly. Finally, understanding how momentum works may give us a better understanding of whether momentum profits are likely to remain strong in the future. Momentum is the only anomaly that has persisted since its widespread publication beginning in the early 1990s. If we can identify deeply ingrained behavioral forces underlying momentum, we might have more reason for believing that momentum profits are likely to continue far into the future.

WHY MOMENTUM WORKS

There are two schools of thought as to why momentum works. The first is that high momentum profits are compensation for assuming greater amounts of risk. This is the rational explanation, which is a matter of cause and effect. If you assume more risk, you should receive more profit as compensation for bearing that risk. It is a view of the world that is in agreement with the idea of rational-based efficient markets. However, since common risk factors such as size and value do not explain momentum profits, we need to find new risk factors that have so far been undiscovered.

The second school of thought is that abnormal momentum profits exist not as compensation for risk, but rather because investors behave unexpectedly and irrationally in systematic and predictable ways. Under the tenets of behavioral finance, markets are not always efficient. It is human behavior that moves markets and not the universal information shared by market participants. Prices do not always reflect all available information because behavioral biases can cause prices to remain too high or too low for long periods of time.

I will explore both the rational and behavioral explanations for momentum. To complicate matters further, some experts say it is possible to characterize momentum profits as a combination of both rational and irrational factors. As we saw in Chapter 3, the real world does not always conform neatly to how we wish to model it.

RATIONAL BASIS FOR MOMENTUM

One of the first attempts at a risk-based explanation for momentum was by Conrad and Kaul (1998). They postulated that cross-sectional variations in expected returns of individual stocks could account for momentum profits. Jegadeesh and Titman (2001), however, found estimation errors in the work of Conrad and Kaul. Jegadeesh and Titman also argued that post-momentum holding period reversals are not consistent with claims that momentum profits come from variations in expected returns. Grundy and Martin (2001) also showed that expected returns from time-varying risk factors do not explain momentum profitability.

RISK-BASED MOMENTUM MODELS

Chordia and Shivakumar (2002) identified some additional risk factors that they hoped would explain momentum profits. These were lagged macroeconomic variables related to the business cycle. Other explanatory risk factors were stochastic, episodic growth shocks, identified by Johnson (2002). Then came nonparametric, stochastic risks related to industry factors described by Ahn, Conrad, and Dittmar (2003), followed by fluctuations in aggregate liquidity identified by Pastor and Stambaugh (2003). Bansal, Dittmar, and Lundbland (2005) identified consumption risk embedded in cash flows, while Sagi and Seasholes (2007) attributed momentum profits to firm-specific attributes like high market-to-book ratio, high revenue volatility, and low cost of goods sold. Liu and Zhang (2008) linked momentum profits to the growth rate of industrial production.

Countering the use of additional risk factors, Griffin, Ji, and Martin (2003) showed that macroeconomic risk variables do not explain momentum profits. Avramov and Chordia (2006) found evidence challenging time-varying macroeconomic variables and liquidity as explanatory variables of momentum. As we will see in a Chapter 9, data mining and overfitting bias also weigh heavily against the search for additional factors that purport to explain momentum on a rational basis.

BEHAVIORAL BASIS FOR MOMENTUM

Fama (1998) suggested that behavioral biases could be subject to "model dredging," where one tries to find biases to fit the facts. He speculated that there might be an increasing number of behavioral models attempting to explain momentum profits. This never happened. In fact, the half dozen or so behavioral explanations for momentum that existed at that time are the same ones that have continued up to the present. Instead, as we just saw, it was the supporters of efficient markets who kept trying to find additional risk factors they hoped would explain momentum on a rational basis. These attempts were similar to the way researchers continued to look for additional risk factors to shore up the problem-prone linear factor models described in Chapter 3.

EARLY BEHAVIORAL MODELING

Social psychology has always had a strong connection with stock market investing. In 1912, Selden wrote *Psychology of the Stock Market*, based on "the belief that the movements of prices on the exchanges are dependent to a very considerable degree on the mental attitude of the investing and trading public." According to Graham and Dodd (1951), "The prices of common stocks are not carefully thought out computations, but the resultants of a welter of human reactions."

The most cited paper to ever appear in the prestigious economics journal *Econometrica* was "Prospect Theory: An Analysis of Decision Under Risk," by two psychologists, Kahneman and Tversky (1979). Kahneman received the Nobel Prize in Economic Sciences in 2002 and the Presidential Medal of Freedom in 2013. (Tversky had passed away earlier.) These authors' groundbreaking paper challenged conventional utility-maximizing behavior. Prospect theory showed that people value gains differently than they value losses. Investors being more sensitive to losses than they are to gains became known as "loss aversion." Prospect theory helped explain why individuals make decisions that can deviate from rational decision making.

The work of Kahneman and Tversky formed the basis for identifying other systematic behavioral biases that express themselves in the following ways:

- Anchoring, insufficient adjustment, underreaction

- Confirmation bias

- Herding, feedback trading, overreaction

- Conservatism, representativeness

- Overconfidence, self-attribution

- Slow diffusion of information

- Disposition effect

ANCHORING AND UNDERREACTION

Anchoring is the tendency to overweight the importance of the first information that we learn. Tversky and Kahneman (1974) demonstrated that people anchor their views to past data and are reluctant to adjust their views to new information. According to Meub and Proeger (2014), anchoring can occur on a social dimension as well on the individual level. Social anchoring can increase pressure toward conformity and acceptance of the status quo.

Anchoring of whatever kind leads to inertia. This can cause investors to underreact to news, which keeps prices below their fair value. Once price trends do finally develop, they remain strong for some time as prices catch up to their fair value.

CONFIRMATION BIAS

Closely related to anchoring is confirmation bias, which is the tendency to overemphasize the importance of information that confirms our views. Confirmation bias is perhaps the oldest known behavioral heuristic. The English philosopher Francis Bacon identified confirmation bias in 1620:

> The human understanding when it once adopted an opinion (either as being the received opinion or as being agreeable to itself) draws all things else to support and agree with it. And though there be a greater number and weight of instances to be found on the other side, yet these it either neglects and despises or else by some distinction sets aside and rejects; in order that by this great and pernicious predetermination the authority of its former conclusions may remain inviolate.

George Orwell stated, "People can foresee the future only when it coincides with their own wishes, and the most grossly obvious facts can be ignored when they are unwelcome." Wason (1960) and Tversky and Kahneman (1974) demonstrated a number of ways in which people look for information that confirms what they already believe while neglecting information that disagrees with their prior beliefs.

Investors subject to confirmation bias who look at recent price moves as representative of the future may invest more in securities that have recently done well and less in those that have not done as well. This can accentuate price trends and lead to their continuation. Friesen, Weller, and Dunham (2009) developed a confirmation bias model that explains the success of technical trading rules using past price patterns.

HERDING, FEEDBACK TRADING, AND OVERREACTION

DeLong et al., (1990) developed the first formal behavioral model to explain momentum profits. Their study identified traders who follow positive feedback strategies, which leads them to buy securities when prices rise and to sell securities when prices fall. This causes price overreaction and subsequent momentum profits. Adding to this effect, Gârleanu and Pedersen (2007) identified risk management schemes using past prices, such as stop-loss orders, which sell in downtrending markets and buy in uptrending markets. These also confirm and reinforce price trends.

Bikhchandani, Hirshleifer, and Welch (1992) described informational cascades that cause traders to jump on the bandwagon where the herding effect feeds upon itself. Herding is also found in equity analysts' recommendations and forecasts (Welch, 2000), in investment newsletters (Graham, 1999), and among institutional investors (Grinblatt, Titman, and Wermers, 1995). John Maynard Keynes identified herding when he said that the prime directive among investment managers is for them to keep their jobs. In order to do this, one should never be wrong on one's own, which creates herding among professional investment managers.

Charles MacKay wrote in his classic book of 1841, *Extraordinary Popular Delusions and the Madness of Crowds*, "Men, it has been well said, think in herds; it will be seen they go mad in herds, while they only recover their senses slowly, and one by one." Herding has a strong physiological, as well as psychological, basis. It is associated with the release of oxytocin and positive feelings of trust and security. Isolation from herds, on the other hand, leads to stimulation of the amygdala neurons, which can trigger a fight-or-flight response and overwhelm the analytical brain.[1]

Herding is primordial. It manifests itself when an animal stays with the crowd in order to reduce its risk of attack. Herding is deeply ingrained in our brain chemistry and DNA.

There is also evidence that market activity can itself stimulate changes in physiology and create additional behavioral changes. Kandasamy et al. (2014) showed that investors experience a sustained increase in the stress hormone cortisol when market volatility increases, which causes them to become more risk-averse. Physiology-induced shifts in risk preferences may be an underappreciated cause of market instability. It may help explain why many individual investors tend to sell in herds at or near market bottoms. It may also give us a better understanding of the basis for feedback-related behavior. We will see in later chapters how absolute and dual momentum can help by removing falling assets from our portfolios before our stress levels become high enough to cause us to behave in ways that are injurious to our financial well-being.

There are several other theories advanced as to why investors follow positive-feedback strategies that lead to herding behavior. Barberis, Shleifer, and Vishny (1998) suggest that investors initially underreact to news due to conservatism. They then overreact over longer periods due to representativeness. In representativeness, as identified by Tversky and Kahneman (1974), you see things that look familiar and draw parallels between events that are not the same. In the case of investors, when they view recent price strength, they may assume it is the harbinger of favorable future economic conditions.

Daniel, Hirshleifer, and Subrahmanyam (1998) propose a feedback model that incorporates investor overconfidence and biased self-attribution. Overconfidence is among the most robust empirical findings in experimental psychology. Kahneman (2011) said, "We are prone to overestimate how much we understand about the world and to underestimate the role of chance in events." Overconfidence can lead to suboptimal outcomes. It is the strongest swimmers who often drown.

Overconfidence also triggers hindsight bias, where individuals believe past events were more predictable than they really were, as well as self-attribution bias. Self-attribution occurs when investors attribute success to their own skills but failures to external factors or bad luck. Investors then buy overconfidently, which pushes up prices. They may afterward overreact to any confirmatory news, which accentuates price trends and sustains positive momentum.

The Barberis et al. (1998) and Daniel et al. (1998) explanations of momentum profits are based on market inefficiencies due to investor behavior. Hong and Stein (1999), on the other hand, attribute momentum profits to market imperfections. They argue that the market contains two types of traders. The first are news watchers who witness the gradual diffusion of news. This leads initially to short-term price underreaction in price movement, which is later reversed. The second type of traders use momentum to take advantage of the profits left behind by the news watchers. They jump on the momentum bandwagon once it gets going in order to profit from the continued diffusion of information. This is how initial underreaction is later followed by delayed overreaction, with investors chasing after returns.

Duffie (2010) attributes slow price movement to investor inattention rather than to the slow diffusion of news. Chan, Jegadeesh, and Lokonishok (2012) say that the reason relative strength momentum works best over 6 to 12 months is that it takes that long for analysts to adjust to new information. Mitchell, Pedersen, and Pulvino (2007) say that market frictions and slow-moving arbitrage capital impede price discovery, which leads to a drop and then a rebound in prices.

DISPOSITION EFFECT

The disposition effect, coined by Shefrin and Statman (1985) and confirmed by Grinblatt and Han (2005), is the tendency of investors to sell their winners too early in order to lock in gains, while holding on to losers too long in the hope of making back what they have lost. Shefrin and Statman attributed this effect to mental accounting (a paper loss is less painful than a realized loss), regret aversion (worrying about doing the wrong thing), lack of self-control (abandoning rules you set for yourself), and tax considerations.

Frazzini (2006) showed that the disposition effect leads to underreaction to news events among mutual fund managers. Asset prices do not immediately rise to their fair value with good news due to premature selling. Similarly, when there is bad news, prices fall less than they should because institutional investors are reluctant to sell. Both of these actions delay the price discovery process, which contributes to the momentum effect as stocks continue trending toward their fundamental value.

Odean (1998), looking at the trading records of 10,000 individual investors in the 1980s, found that investors sell stocks for a gain 50% more frequently than they sell stocks for a loss. He found that the disposition effect costs investors, on average, 4.4% in annual returns.

PUTTING IT ALL TOGETHER

The behavioral explanations for momentum focus on human emotional biases that cause markets to display initial underreaction followed by delayed overreaction. The disposition effect impedes an asset's rise to true value due to premature selling and to buying inertia. Anchoring and confirmation bias can also keep prices from reflecting their true values.

Longer term, there is a catch-up process that subsequently leads to overreaction through herding behavior and the bandwagon effect. Thus, herding/anchoring/confirmation bias and the disposition effect complement each other and can lead to a unified, behaviorally based concept of momentum-inducing behavior.

Now, if someone asks you why momentum works, you too might just stare blankly at him or her. You may be at a loss for words to explain it, but at least you now should know that momentum is not just a 212-year flash in the pan. There are logical reasons why momentum works—and, in fact, there are plenty of them.

Some of those reasons may, at this point, seem obscure and vague. There is a recommended reading list at the end of the book for those who would like to explore behavioral finance in more detail.[2] Keep in mind that when someone asked Richard Thaler about the choice between accepting the idea of efficient markets or behavioral finance, his response was, "It's a choice between being precisely wrong or vaguely right."[3]

If you accept the behavioral basis for momentum, you should be glad that behavioral biases are firmly grounded in our psychological makeup and physiology. This makes it unlikely that they will change in the future. You might also take comfort in the idea that momentum lets us profit from human behavioral biases instead of being subject to them in adverse ways.

Now that we have these theoretical underpinnings out of the way, it is time to move on to matters that are more practical. We will next look at potential assets we might include in our momentum portfolio.

CHAPTER 5

ASSET SELECTION:
THE GOOD, THE BAD,
AND THE UGLY

> Diversification is protection against ignorance. Wide diversification
> is only required when investors do not understand what they
> are doing.
>
> —*Warren Buffett*

W E ALL WANT AN INVESTMENT that will capture the highest possible risk premium while minimizing tail risk or drawdown. Risk
premium is the reward we receive for the risks associated with a buy-and-
hold strategy. In the preface to his classic book, *Stocks for the Long Run,*
Jeremy Siegel (2014) writes, "over long periods of time, the returns on
equities not only surpassed those on all other financial assets, but were far
safer and more predictable than bond returns when inflation was taken
into account."

From 1900 through 2013, U.S. equities returned an average annualized 6.5% premium over the risk-free rate, while non-U.S. equities
offered a 4.5% risk premium.[1] During the past 30-year bond bull market,
bond returns have just about kept pace with equities. However, this has
not always been the case.

BONDS? WE DON'T NEED NO STINKIN' BONDS

The average annualized real return after inflation on U.S. long-term government bonds from 1900 through 2013 was just 1.9%, considerably less than the 6.5% average annualized real return from U.S. equities during this same period.[2] Bonds had negative real returns from 1940 all the way through 1981. Purchasers of long-term government bonds in 1941 had to wait until 1991 before breaking even.

As for what we can reasonably expect now, current bond yield is a good indicator of what you can expect to earn in the future. John Bogle, founder and former chairperson of The Vanguard Group, pointed out that since 1926, the yield on 10-year U.S. Treasury notes explains 92% of the annualized return an investor would have earned had one held the notes to maturity and reinvested the interest payments at prevailing rates. The current annual yield on 10-year Treasury notes is 2.7%. This is the best guess of what holders of intermediate-term Treasury bonds can expect as a reasonable annual return now.

Historically, investors have used bonds to diversify their stock portfolios and to reduce portfolio volatility. Investors typically set aside enough in lower-volatility assets, such as bonds, to enable them to weather periodic stock market downturns. During the 2007–2008 financial crises, bonds held up relatively well with respect to stocks. However, that has not always been the case. Stocks and bonds have been positively correlated nearly 70% of the time since 1973. They share some common risk factors and move in opposite directions only under certain conditions. Figure 5.1 shows the five-year rolling correlation between the Ibbotson Long-Term U.S. Government Bond Index and the S&P 500 Stock Index since 1931. You can see that the correlation between stocks and government bonds has been greater than zero more than half the time.[3]

Bonds can also be less stable than stocks and just as vulnerable to extreme losses. Since 1900, the maximum drawdown in real terms of long-term U.S. government bonds was 68%. The maximum drawdown for U.S. stocks was 73%. For every five-year period since 1807, the worst

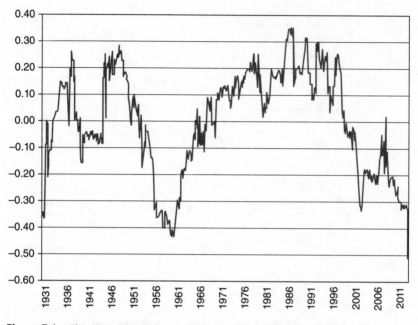

Figure 5.1   Five-Year Correlations Between the S&P 500 Index and U.S. Government Bonds, 1931–2011

performance of stocks (–11% per year) was only slightly worse than the worst five-year performance for bills and bonds. When looking at 10-year holding periods, the worst stock performance was actually better than the worst bond performance![4]

Looking at returns rather than losses over the past 200+ years, the real return from bonds has averaged 3.6% annually, while the real return from stocks has averaged 6.6% per year.[5] Figure 5.2 shows what this has meant for investors over the long run. I suggest staring at this chart until the message really sinks in. Your long-term financial condition may depend on it. When matched up with bonds, bills, and commodities (gold), stocks are by far the big winner in terms of long-run cumulative return.

Only about half of U.S. households hold equities, including what they have as retirement assets. In their paper "Myopic Loss Aversion and the Equity Premium Puzzle," Bernartzi and Thaler (1995) make the case that investors do not hold more stocks relative to bonds because investors

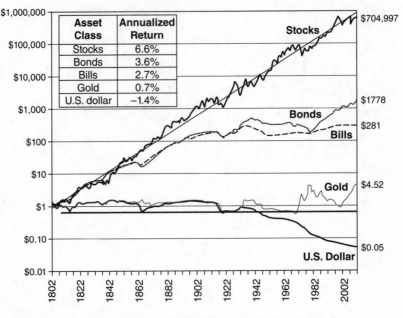

Figure 5.2   Real Returns: Stocks, Bonds, Bills, Gold, and the U.S. Dollar, 1802–2012

(Source: Jeremy Siegel, Stocks for the Long Run)

focus too much on short-term performance and volatility instead of long-term performance goals. This loss aversion leads to reduced stock holdings, lower stock prices, and increased equity risk premiums. By focusing more on the big picture and less on short-term volatility, one may be able to stay in the markets longer term and capture this high equity risk premium. As we will see in later chapters, the risk-reducing nature of absolute and dual momentum can help make this goal a reality.

Since bonds have performed well over the past 30 years, many investors may have forgotten that the last bond bear market lasted all the way from 1946 to 1981. It culminated in intermediate Treasury yields rising to over 15%. Figure 5.3 shows where we are now in relation to the long-term history of the bond market, as per the Robert Shiller website.[6]

Given the way that bond prices move inversely to interest rate changes, intermediate-term bonds could lose half their value if their annual yield

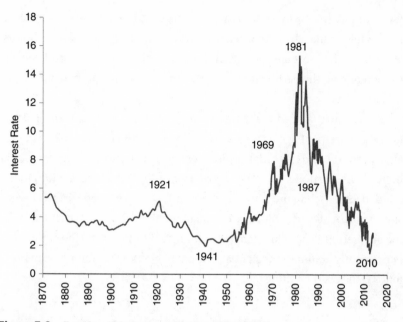

Figure 5.3   Ten-Year U.S. Treasury Yields, 1871–2013

rises to their long-run average rate of 6.75%. One should keep in mind that real Treasury bond returns were negative for the next 45 years following similar valuation levels as exist today.

Here is what Warren Buffett wrote about fixed-income investing in his 2012 annual letter to Berkshire Hathaway, Inc., shareholders:

> They are among the most dangerous of assets. Over the past century these instruments have destroyed the purchasing power of investors in many countries, even as these holders continued to receive timely payments of interest and principal. . . . Right now, bonds should come with a warning label.

The question then is should one ever have a permanent allocation to bonds when absolute (and dual) momentum can reduce the downside exposure of a stock portfolio? Absolute momentum uses bonds, but only when stocks are weak and bonds are strong. Bonds were valuable in 2008, for example, when stocks were down sharply. A dynamic asset allocation methodology like absolute momentum will utilize either stocks or bonds, but only at the most appropriate times. It can give the best of both worlds while reducing the performance drag that comes from a permanent allocation to bonds.

Later I will show how conservative investors, such as those past or nearing retirement age or with a strong aversion to risk, can use a modest allocation to bonds in order to dampen the short-run volatility of a dual momentum portfolio. I will also show how to apply dual momentum to the bond market itself in order to enhance bond returns and reduce their downside exposure. Due to cognitive dissonance and anchoring bias, it may take the next serious bear market in bonds for investors to give up the notion that permanently holding a substantial amount of bonds in their long-term portfolios is the prudent thing to do.

RISK PARITY, REALLY?

In recent years, some investors have been looking in the opposite direction by greatly increasing their fixed-income exposure. There are a number of "risk parity" programs that hold more than 75% of their portfolios in bonds in order to equalize stock and bond volatility.[7] Because bonds return less than stocks, these programs often use leverage to boost their expected returns back up to acceptable levels. This may not be such a good idea, given that interest rates are now near historic lows. Risk in leveraged portfolios has many facets, such as kurtosis (fat tails), illiquidity, counterparty, and contagion risk. Negative skewness (negative returns being larger in magnitude than positive returns) can be especially harmful when combined with leverage. Risk parity investors may just be exchanging equities-based risk for other forms of risk that can be equally as problematic.

In the second quarter of 2013, Invesco's $23.5 billion Balanced-Risk Allocation strategy fell 5.5%. The largest risk parity program, Bridgewater's $79 billion All Weather Fund, had a loss of 8.4% on $56 billion of inflation-linked debt, forcing it to reevaluate its heavy reliance on fixed income. In contrast to this, when using dual momentum "we don't need no stinkin' bonds," except when dual momentum tells us that we do. We utilize bonds when they are in the best position to add value to our portfolio instead of being a likely drag on portfolio performance.

FIFTY-SEVEN VARIETIES OF DIVERSIFICATION

Diversification is an age-old concept. It showed up in the Babylonian Talmud 1,500 years ago: "A man should always place his money one-third in land, a third in merchandise, and keep a third ready to hand." Ecclesiastes 11:2 tells us to "divide your portion to seven or even eight, for you do not know what misfortune may occur on earth." In *The Merchant of Venice*, Shakespeare wrote, "My ventures are not in one bottom trusted, nor to one place; nor is my whole estate upon the fortune of the present year. Therefore, my merchandise makes me not sad."

The impetus toward greater diversification got a big boost following the global financial crisis of 2007–2008 with its severe drawdown across many asset classes. A popular saying is that diversification works well . . . until it does not. Correlations tend to rise sharply during periods of market stress, which is when diversification is needed the most. This has led to an even greater impetus toward diversification.

INTERNATIONAL DIVERSIFICATION

A common way to diversify U.S. stock market exposure other than with bonds is to hold foreign stocks. International mutual funds have been available to U.S. investors since the 1960s, and international diversification started to catch on among U.S. institutional investors beginning in the 1970s.[8]

From 1900 through 2012, the annual risk premium of U.S. stocks over Treasury bills averaged 6.5%. For 18 non-U.S. markets, it averaged 4.5%.[9] Long-run returns of U.S. stocks have been substantially better than the returns of non-U.S. stocks. Correlations between U.S and non-U.S. stocks have risen in recent years. The average 12-month correlation between the S&P 500 and the MSCI EAFE from 1971 through 1999 was 0.42. Since then, it has averaged 0.83. Looking at the 50 largest U.S. companies, the median firm now conducts 57% of its business outside the United States.

The diversification value of U.S. and foreign equities has definitely diminished. However, given the way different markets come in and out of favor, non-U.S. stocks may still add value to a portfolio based on relative strength momentum. This is why we include them in our dual momentum portfolio.

EMERGING MARKETS

In the quest for additional diversification and higher possible returns, some investors utilize emerging market equities and treat them as a separate asset class. There are, however, additional risks associated with emerging markets. They have less than 30 years of price history, are sometimes thin and illiquid, and are more expensive to trade and to manage. Accounting methods in developing countries are also not always up to the standards used in developed countries.

Because emerging markets can suffer sharp and rapid price declines, you often see them aggregated into baskets that trade as a group. This stems from the belief that diversification among emerging markets will reduce their risk. However, baskets of emerging market stocks create contagion risk, causing them to trade together as a whole. Aggregation and contagion can also amplify liquidity risk. During the Russian debt crisis, emerging markets as far away as Singapore suffered major capital outflows and extreme price volatility.

Due to increased globalization, correlations are higher now among emerging markets, as well as between emerging and developed markets. Figure 5.4 shows the five-year rolling monthly correlations between emerging and developed markets. It was below 0.30 in the 1990s. However, for the past three years the correlation has remained steady at over 0.90.

From a diversification point of view, emerging markets have lost much of their appeal. What they mostly add now is additional volatility and uncertainty, which is generally undesirable. We include emerging assets in our dual momentum–based model by virtue of their natural inclusion in the non-U.S. equity index portion of our portfolio. Since that index is capitalization weighted, emerging markets make up only 14% of that index. We could easily drop emerging markets entirely from our dual momentum portfolio without a significant dilution in our results.

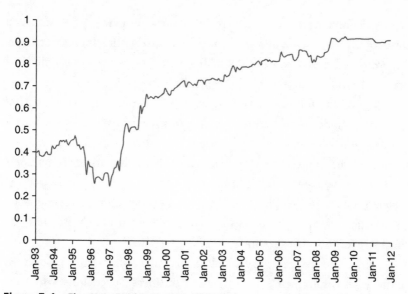

Figure 5.4   **Five-Year Rolling Monthly EAFE Versus Emerging Market Correlations**

PASSIVE COMMODITY FUTURES

Another volatile asset class that has attracted a considerable following in recent years is commodity futures. One reason for this is the belief that commodities act as an inflation hedge. Yet common stocks over the long run, Treasury Inflation-Protected Securities (TIPS), and even Treasury bills can also serve as a hedge against inflation.

The underlying problem with commodity futures is that they, like currencies, are not an asset class in the same sense as stocks and bonds.[10] An asset class is a portfolio of homogeneous assets delivering a positive excess return above the risk-free rate in the long run, corresponding to a "risk premium" or reward for the risk associated with holding that asset.

Stocks and bonds exist as vehicles for raising capital. In return for this, investors can expect streams of payments from bonds or residual cash flow from equities. However, one cannot generally expect a long-only position in commodity futures to provide an excess return, as is the case with stocks and bonds.

Commodity futures contracts are a zero sum game in which the profits and losses of contract buyers and sellers are equal, disregarding transaction costs. According to Erb and Harvey (2006), "The average excess returns of individual commodity futures contracts have been indistinguishable from zero."

Commodity futures are an insurance-type market where hedgers and speculators trade risks. There is no expectation of aggregate positive returns. Futures contracts cease to exist on their expiration dates, and there is no wealth created in these transactions. Because gains and losses are symmetrical to the buyer and seller of a futures contract, one cannot say that the buyer, by taking on volatility, is entitled to a positive return, since the seller, by the same reasoning, would also be entitled to a fair return. One of them must lose for the other to gain.

Commercial hedgers are generally short sellers who need to lay off risks of the unknown in their capital-intensive business. Speculators, who have no actual need to participate in commodity markets, traditionally take the other sides of these trades because of the premiums they receive as they roll expiring futures contracts out to longer maturities.

In the 1980s, when I was managing large commodity pools, buyers of commodity futures enjoyed a systematic positive return called the "roll yield" or "roll premium" that flowed from hedgers to speculators. Hedgers would pay what amounted to an insurance premium to speculators in order to shed themselves of the risks that they were unwilling or unable to bear.

However, those dynamics have now changed. Using data only through the early 2000s that showed aggregate commodities to be a decent portfolio diversifier, academic papers like the one by Gorton and Rouwenhorst (2006) induced many institutional investors to invest in portfolios of passive commodity futures. Goldman Sachs and other indexers promoted commodity futures as a new asset class suitable for institutional investors.

Spurred on by a nearly 150% increase in the value of a basket of commodities from 2002 through 2007, over $100 billion poured into the commodity futures market from 2004 through 2008. This caused the "financialization" of commodities. According to J.P. Morgan's Commodities Research, by the end of 2009 investors had linked $55 billion to the Goldman Sachs Commodity Index (GSCI) and $30 billion to the Dow Jones-UBS Commodity Index (DJ-UBSCI).

Commodity investments more than doubled from roughly $170 billion in July 2007 to $410 billion in February 2013. Endowments, pension funds, hedge funds, risk parity programs, and the public have all joined the bandwagon and scrambled to add long-only commodity index futures in an effort to diversify their portfolios.

Many pension programs now believe they should have 5 to 10% of their portfolio assets committed to commodities. As shown in Figure 5.5, from 1990 through 2012, the share of open interest in commodity futures contracts held by noncommercial interests increased from 15% to 42%.[11]

These new speculators tend to go long regardless of price. As the number of insurance providers (speculators) became increasingly large compared to the number of insurance buyers (hedgers), the roll yield dissipated and is now negative. From 1969 to 1992, the roll return averaged 11% per year. Since 2001, it has averaged a negative 6.6%.[12]

The cumulative roll yield gain that existed up to 1970 was all lost by the end of 2009. Passive commodities indexes are still below their high-water marks reached in 2008. The odds are now stacked against those who hold long commodity futures. Yet passive commodities are still widely touted as a desirable portfolio diversifier.

Figure 5.5   Percentage of Open Interest Held by Noncommercials

(Source: Adam Zaremba)

Several newer commodity indexes, like the Deutsche Bank Liquid Commodity Index Optimum Yield or the SummerHaven Dynamic indexes, try to reduce the roll yield disadvantage by selectively seeking futures contracts, when possible, that still offer a positive roll premium. However, passive commodity index funds, regardless of their roll premium capture inclinations, face another formidable obstacle: front-running costs that come from regularly rolling over their commodity futures positions. They occur when others anticipate and trade in front of the futures rollover dates, then take profits afterward.

Yiqun Mou (2011) estimates that front-running costs were 3.6% annually from January 2000 through March 2010. J.P. Morgan Commodities Research reported in 2009 that roll returns have put a drag of 3% to 4% per year on commodity index returns since 1991. These hidden costs can quickly take the wind out of the sails of the buyers of passive commodities index futures.

Rising correlations are another problem associated with commodities. According to Tang and Xiong (2012), the average one-year rolling correlation among indexed commodities was at a stable level below 0.10 throughout the 1990s and 2000s. By 2009, it had climbed to 0.50. Before 2008, the correlation between the GSCI and the S&P 500 was generally in a band between −0.20 and 0.10. Since then, it has shot up to over 0.50 and has generally remained there.[13]

Furthermore, during both the 1929 stock market crash and the 2008 financial crisis, the correlation between equities and commodities shot up to over 80%. Commodities diversification was lacking when it was needed the most. According to Lombardi and Ravazzolo (2013) of the Bank for International Settlements, the popular view that commodities should be included in one's portfolio as a hedging device is no longer valid.[14]

The decrease in roll return and increase in return correlation now render the mean-variance diversification benefit of a passive allocation to commodity futures insignificant. A comprehensive study by Daskalaki and Skiadopoulos (2011) called "Should Investors Include Commodities in Their Portfolios After All? New Evidence," revealed that the introduction of commodity instruments in a traditional stock/bond portfolio is no longer beneficial for a utility-maximizing investor. Blitz and de Groot (2004) also found that commodities deserve little or no role in a stock/bond portfolio, although a case could be made for including momentum, carry, and low-volatility commodity market risk factors.

Table 5.1   Dow Jones UBS Commodity Index 1991–2013

	DJ-UBSCI	S&P 500	MSCI EAFE	MSCI EM	AGG BOND
Annual return	4.1	9.9	6.5	10.3	6.4
Annual std dev	18.2	18.6	20.2	35.5	5.1

The first year that investors could actually include a passive commodity index in their portfolios was 1991. Table 5.1 shows the performance of the DJ-UBSCI, compared with the performance of the S&P 500, Morgan Stanley Capital International Europe, Australasia, and Far East (MSCI EAFE), MSCI Emerging Markets (MSCI EM), and Barclays Capital U. S. Aggregate Bond indexes from 1991 through 2013.[15] This includes the 2002–2007 period that was very favorable to commodities. Figure 5.6 shows visually the DJ-UBSCI versus the S&P 500.

Longer term, from January 1975 through December 2011, the GSCI (DJ-UBSCI was not available before 1991) had an annual average return of 6.1% with a standard deviation of 19.3%, while five-year Treasury bonds had a 7.7% return and a 4.3% standard deviation.

Figure 5.6   Dow Jones-UBS Commodity Index Versus S&P 500 Index

MANAGED COMMODITY FUTURES

Much of what I said about passive commodities is also applicable to actively managed commodity futures. Managed futures typically use trend-following methods to participate on both the long and the short side of the commodity futures markets. However, any excess return earned from actively managed futures trading is still dependent on capturing risk premium from commercial hedgers, or it comes from the difficult task of outsmarting other speculators.

In the 1980s, when I successfully managed commodity pools, there was an abundance of roll premium available for speculators. This allowed many commodity-trading advisors to prosper. In recent years, however, many more speculators have entered the marketplace to compete with one another for the same trend-following profits. This has made it much more difficult to earn attractive risk-adjusted returns. The situation is now similar to active stock management, where those with the same information are competing with one another to gain an edge. With equities, however, there is an upward drift in stock prices and a proven risk premium. This is, unfortunately, not the case with commodities.

Despite these sobering facts, according to Barclays Hedge, the amount of assets in managed futures grew from $50.9 billion in 2007 to $325 billion in 2014. This accounts for 15% of the entire hedge fund industry. What is especially surprising about this is that the average managed futures return since 2007 has been negative with the rolling annual return being negative now for 21 straight months.

It could be that increased participation in managed futures has much to do with the propensity of institutional investors to diversify aggressively in recent years no matter what the consequences. The average U.S. college endowment fund, for example, now has 54% of its assets in alternative investments and only 15% in U.S. stocks. Sovereign funds have also greatly stepped up their allocations to alternatives. I call this the "everything but the kitchen sink" approach to investing. So what exactly has happened with managed futures since this onslaught of additional capital?

Bhardwaj, Gorton, and Rouwenhorst (2013) have a paper appropriately named "Fooling Some of the People All of the Time: The Inefficient Performance and Persistence of Commodity Trading Advisors." They found using the equal-weighted performance of the Lipper-TASS database of 930 commodity trading advisors (CTAs), after adjusting for survivorship and backfill bias, that CTA excess returns to investors over U.S. Treasury bills averaged only 1.8% per year from 1994 through 2012 (see Figure 5.7).[16] This was not significantly different from zero.

As with other hedge funds, CTA fees are often 2% of assets and 20% of profits each year. During this period, aggregate CTA fees averaged 4.3% per year, which was more than twice what investors received. Investors had earned returns not much greater than Treasury bills while taking on volatility equal to equities. Bhardwaj et al. (2013) concluded that interest in managed futures has remained strong because investors' experience of poor performance is not common knowledge. This does not speak well for due diligence these days.

Research into actual futures trading since the mid-1980s has confirmed the lack of profitability using quantitative timing strategies. Marshall, Cahan, and Cahan (2008) applied over 7,000 trading rules in five rule families (filter rules, moving averages, support and resistance, channel breakouts, and on-balance volume) to 15 major commodity markets from 1984 through 2005. Using two different bootstrapping methodologies and accounting for

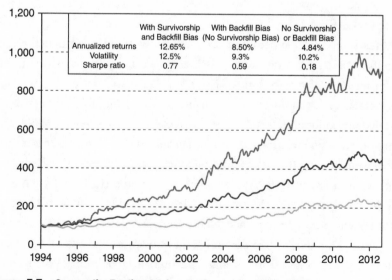

Figure 5.7   Commodity Trading Advisor Performance, 1994–2012

(Source: Bhardwaj, Gorton, and Rouwenhorst)

data-snooping bias, the authors found that these rules were not profitable on their own, despite their wide following.

Managed futures might still find a place in some portfolios due to their diversification value. In 2008, the Credit Suisse Managed Futures Index was up 17.6% (this was the last year that managed futures showed a gain), while the Credit Suisse Hedge Fund Index was down 20.7%. During this time, the Reuters/CRB Commodity Index was down 23.7%, the S&P 500 Index was down 38.4%, the MSCI World Index was down 42.1%, and the Dow Jones Wilshire Real Estate Securities Index was down 43.1%. Commodities can hedge supply shocks to the economy, such as the oil embargo of 1973–1974, but not usually overall shocks to the economy, such as the recessions of 1981 and 2001.

There is an alternative for those still wanting to include actively managed futures in their portfolios. Using data from 58 liquid futures markets from June 1985 to June 2012, Hurst, Ooi, and Pedersen (2014) were able to achieve comparable before-costs CTA results using a simple, trend-following absolute momentum strategy similar to the one you will see in Chapter 8. Those who want to participate in actively managed commodity futures can avoid high fees (and achieve trends with benefits) by implementing this kind of simple, trend-following strategy.

HEDGE FUNDS

Alfred Winslow Jones became a U.S. diplomat working in Berlin in the early 1930s, where he also ran secret missions for a clandestine anti-Nazi group. During his earlier years, Jones traveled and drank with Ernest Hemingway, then later earned a doctorate in sociology from Columbia University. He joined the editorial staff at *Fortune* magazine in the early 1940s. While writing an article on investment trends for *Fortune* in 1948, Jones had the unique idea of managing the risk of holding long stock positions by selling short other stocks and using leverage to boost portfolio returns. In 1949, at the age of 48, Jones raised $60,000 from four friends, added it to $40,000 of his own money, and began the first "hedged fund," as he called it.

In 1952, Jones opened the fund to new investors and altered the structure by converting it from a general partnership to a limited partnership. He also added a 20% incentive fee as compensation for himself as managing partner. He modeled his profit participation idea after the Phoenician merchants who kept one-fifth of the profits from successful voyages. As the first money manager to combine short selling, leverage, shared risk through a partnership with other investors, and a compensation system based on investment performance, Jones became the father of all hedge funds.

The hedge fund industry did not really get off the ground until 1966, when an article in *Fortune* magazine highlighted how Jones's obscure private investment fund had outperformed every mutual fund by high double digits over the prior five years. In the 10 years leading up to 1965, Jones had earned almost twice as much as his nearest competitor. Two years after the *Fortune* article, there were almost 200 hedge funds.

In an effort to maximize returns (and performance fees), many funds turned away from Jones' long/short hedged strategy but retained the leverage feature. Hedge funds moved increasingly away from the theme of Conrad Thomas' 1970s book (with the best title ever given an investment book), *Hedgemanship: How to Make Money in Bear Markets, Bull Markets, and Chicken Markets While Confounding Professional Money Managers and Attracting a Better Class of Women*. Doing away with the hedged feature led to very large losses and many hedge fund closures during each bear market. The 1973–1974 market crash, in fact, wiped out most hedge funds. According to research firm Tremont Partners Inc., there were only 84 hedge funds in 1984.

The industry continued this way, remaining relatively quiet until a 1986 article in *Institutional Investor* touted the double-digit returns of Julian Robertson's Tiger Fund. Investors quickly started flocking to hedge funds again. Lured by the 2% of assets and 20% of profits fee structure, high-profile money managers deserted the mutual fund industry in droves during the early 1990s to seek fame and fortune as hedge fund managers.

The industry was hard hit by the collapse of Long-Term Capital Management in 1998, followed by the spectacular implosions of Robertson's Tiger Funds and the high-flying Quantum Fund in 2000. In 2002, the well-known money manager Mario Gabelli called hedge funds "a highly speculative vehicle for unwitting fat cats and careless financial institutions to lose their shirts."

Managed futures are but one category of hedge fund. There are 18 others, the majority of which are long only. Drawn like moths to a flame by their strong desires to enhance performance and diversify more broadly, institutions have greatly stepped up their hedge fund investments. At the end of 2011, 61% of the worldwide investment in hedge funds came from institutional sources. Hedge fund assets as a whole grew from $60 billion in 1990 to $200 billion in 1999 and were at an all-time high of more than $2.7 trillion in the first quarter of 2014.

Looking at hedge fund performance as of December 2013, the Bloomberg Hedge Funds Aggregate Index was down 1.8% from its July 2007 peak. This marked the eleventh consecutive year in which the performance of a balanced 60/40 stock/bond portfolio beat the hedge fund industry.

The average hedge fund has lagged the performance of the S&P 500 Index since 1995. This may be acceptable for hedge funds that actually do hedge, but most of them do not. In a study of 306 long-only hedge fund returns from 1986 through 2000, Griffin and Xu (2009) found that hedge funds have no special abilities to generate positive, risk-adjusted excess returns. Since then, hedge fund alpha has remained negative.

Funds of funds that hold other hedge funds (FOFs) have done no better. Dewaele et al. (2011) studied 1,315 FOFs in the Lipper-TASS database from 1994 through August 2009. After adjusting for risk factors, they found that only 5.6% of FOFs showed risk-adjusted returns greater than the hedge fund indexes, and there was no significant difference between the average FOF and a fund picked at random.

Simon Lack, author of the 2012 book *The Hedge Fund Mirage*, used the BarclaysHedge database from 1998 through 2010 to perform asset-weighted return calculations, similar to an internal rate of return. He argued that this is more appropriate than the usual time-weighted return calculation because hedge fund managers have control over when they accept and commit capital. Using this asset-weighted return measure, the HFR Global Hedge Fund Index returned only 2.1% annualized those 12 years. After adjusting for fees charged by FOFs and for survivorship and backfill biases, Lack estimated that from 1998 through 2010 investors collectively lost $308 billion, while the hedge fund industry earned fees of $324 billion. According to Lack, hedge funds have taken 84% of investor profits since 1998, funds of funds have taken 14% of profits, and only 2% has gone to investors. Lack further noted that if all the money ever invested in hedge funds had instead been put in Treasury bills, investors would have been twice as well off.

Dichev and Yu (2009) conducted a similar study using dollar-weighted hedge fund returns from 1980 through 2008. They found that dollar-weighted returns were 3 to 7% lower than buy-and-hold returns. Using factor models for risk, the authors found the real alpha of hedge funds to be close to zero. In absolute terms, weighted hedge fund returns were reliably lower than the return on the S&P 500 index.

Not only have hedge fund returns been lacking but also hedge fund risks have been high due to high leverage, lack of transparency, and limited liquidity. Castle Hall Alternatives, which maintains a database of hedge fund frauds and blowups, reports more than 300 frauds and implosions over the past decade. The average hedge fund lifespan has been about five years. Out of an estimated 7,200 hedge funds that existed in 2010, 775 failed or closed in 2011, 873 in 2012, and 914 in 2013. Within those three years, around one-third of all funds disappeared with new ones taking their place.

Hedge fund diversification value has also been declining. According to Deutsche Bank, the average correlation of hedge funds to the S&P 500 (based on monthly returns over a four-year rolling window) has risen from under 0.50 in the mid-1990s to over 0.80 now. Fourteen of the 18 hedge fund strategies suffered their worst-ever drawdown at the same time in 2008, despite their pursuing what appeared to be different strategies in different markets.

With standard annual fees of 2% of assets and 20% of profits, hedge funds distinguish themselves more as a compensation structure than as an asset class. Collectively, the top 25 hedge fund managers regularly earn more than the combined compensation of all 500 CEOs of the S&P 500. Hedge fund managers, in aggregate, have captured most or all of any excess return and have given little or none of it to investors. According to Warren Buffett, "A number of smart people are involved in running hedge funds. But to a great extent their efforts are self-neutralizing, and their IQ will not overcome the costs they impose on investors. Investors, on average and over time, will do better with a low-cost index fund."

PRIVATE EQUITY

Private equity encompasses several long-term illiquid investment strategies. It began as a rebranding of leveraged buyouts after the 1980s. Private equity also includes venture capital, private growth capital, and distressed capital/ special situations. The amount of private equity assets under management in 2012 was around $2 trillion, comparable to the amount in hedge funds.

Buyout funds have been much riskier than the S&P 500 and have historically had significantly higher excess returns. However, according to Higson and Stucke (2012), there has been a downward trend in buyout fund absolute returns over the 28 years ending in 2008. The excess returns of buyout funds have been driven largely by the performance of the top 10% of these funds. It would have been difficult to know ahead of time which ones these were going to be.

Over the past 40 years, venture capital funds have had annual gains of 13.4%, versus 12.4% for the S&P 500 Index and 14.4% for the S&P SmallCap Growth Index. Venture capital funds have had higher volatility, illiquidity, and survivorship risk. Only 60% to 75% of venture capital funds have survived more than 10 years. According to Harris, Jenkinson, and Kaplan (2013), since 2000 the average venture capital fund has underperformed public markets by about 5% over the life of the fund.

From 2001 to 2010, U.S. pension plans, on average, made 4.5% after fees from their investments in private equity funds. They paid an average of 4% each year in management fees, plus 20% of profits. This means fees amounted to about 70% of gross investment performance. Private equity funds usually require a five- to seven-year lockup period of invested capital. They have also been subject to widespread complaints of publishing inaccurate valuations.

Despite high fees, illiquidity, and variable performance, private equity is, by far, the Yale endowment's largest asset allocation. Endowments, in general, are among the most prominent investors in private equity and hedge funds. Private equity funds, like hedge funds, are best left to institutional investors having superior due diligence capabilities. Even these investors may want to reconsider their level of commitment to these alternative investments. Barber and Wang (2011) did a 20-year study of university endowment performance from 1991 through 2011. They found that for the average endowment, factor models with only stock and bond benchmarks explain virtually all of the time-series variation in their returns and show no alpha.

ACTIVELY MANAGED MUTUAL FUNDS

We have seen that it is difficult for investors to profit from funds that charge annual fees of 2% of assets and 20% of profits, such as managed futures, hedge funds, and private equity. Let us look now at other forms of active management that do not charge such high fees.

More than 52 million households own mutual funds. Total U.S. assets in mutual funds now exceed $11.6 trillion. According to the Investment Company Institute (ICI), index funds make up 17.4% of domestic equity mutual funds, while actively managed equity funds make up 82.6%.

Researchers have extensively studied the performance of actively managed mutual funds since the 1960s. Jensen (1968) helped passive management gain a foothold with his study showing that the average mutual fund from 1945 through 1964 did no better than buying and holding the market.

Survivorship bias was a significant issue in these early studies. Through 2012, only 51% of actively managed mutual funds had survived over the preceding 10 years. One of the first comprehensive studies of mutual fund performance that considered survivorship bias was by Malkiel (1995). He found that, in aggregate, equity mutual funds from 1971 through 1991 underperformed their benchmark portfolios, both after and before management expenses.

Fama and French (2009) picked up where Malkiel left off. Using mutual fund data from 1984 through 2006, they discovered that few actively managed funds produced benchmark-adjusted returns sufficient to cover their costs, and it was hard to tell whether good performance was due to skill or to luck. The only thing predictable was that actively managed funds with high fees underperformed those with low fees, and both underperformed index funds having the lowest fees.

In a similar study, Barras, Scaillet, and Wermers (2010) studied 2,076 U.S. mutual funds from 1989 through 2006. Adjusting for data snooping bias, they concluded that the number of funds with skilled managers where active returns exceeded costs was statistically indistinguishable from zero.[17] They also found that the fraction of skilled managers declined from 14.40% to 0.60% from 1989 to 2006. The authors attributed this shift in performance to an increase in unskilled managers who nonetheless charged high fees with funds having high expense ratios.

According to Morningstar, the average annual expense ratio of an actively managed mutual fund is 1.41%, compared to 0.20% for a passively managed fund. Actively managed funds also have, on average, a portfolio turnover ratio of 83%, which adds an additional 0.70% per year in transactions cost expense. Furthermore, tax inefficiencies can add an additional 1% per year to the costs of owning an actively managed fund. Not accounting for possible negative tax consequences, Morningstar reported that at the end of 2012, after adjusting for survivorship bias, over 80% of large-blend mutual funds underperformed their benchmarks over the past 3, 5, 10, and 15 years.

Credit Suisse reported that the annual total return of the S&P 500 Index for the last 20 years ending in 2013 was 9.3%. The average actively managed mutual fund during this period earned 1.0% to 1.5% less than that, due to its expense ratios and transaction costs. The average returns investors earned was another 1% to 2% less than that, due to poor timing decisions. The overall return for investors in actively managed funds was 60% to 80% less than the market return over the past 20 years.[18] According to John Bogle, founder and former CEO of The Vanguard Group (now the world's largest mutual fund company), "Selecting funds that will significantly exceed market returns, a search in which hope springs eternal and in which past performance has proven of virtually no predictive value, is a loser's game."

Vanguard has an interactive website where you can input an active fund's expense ratio and see how your capital would grow at a 6% growth rate, compared to an index fund with an expense ratio of 0.25%.[19] If we input the average annual active fund expense ratio of 1.41%, at the end of 50 years we will have accumulated less than half the profits we would from using a low-cost index fund.

Warren Buffett once said:

> Most investors, both institutional and individual, will find that the best way to own common stocks is through an index fund that charges minimal fees. Those following this path are sure to beat the net results (after fees and expenses) delivered by the great majority of investment professionals.[20]

Buffett puts his own money where his mouth is. Buffett's Berkshire Hathaway stock will go to charity after his death. For his heirs, Buffett has instructed the trustees of his estate to place 10% of what remains into short-term government bonds and 90% into a low-cost S&P 500 Index fund.

Researchers have been saying for many years that actively managed mutual funds offer no aggregate advantage over passively managed index funds. Passive index funds that were nonexistent in 1975 now account for almost 30% of the investment fund market. Yet actively managed funds still have more than twice the assets as passively managed ones.

OTHER ACTIVE INVESTMENT MANAGEMENT

There is more money actively managed outside than inside mutual funds. *Pensions & Investments* reported that the top 500 global asset managers held $62 trillion in assets under management in 2011, while the Investment Company Institute reported worldwide mutual fund assets of $23.8 trillion that same year. As for active investment management performance outside mutual funds, Busse, Goyal, and Wahal (2010) studied 4,617 domestic equity institutional products managed by 1,448 investment management firms from 1991 through 2008. They found risk-adjusted returns of these managers to be statistically indistinguishable from zero. The fees for active management came to 100% of the incremental returns earned over widely available passive alternatives. In the words of Eugene Fama, "After taking risk into account, do more managers than you'd see by chance outperform with persistence? Virtually every economist who studied this question answers with a resounding 'no.'"

Whether through mutual funds or managed accounts, there is, in aggregate, little or no reward for bearing the additional costs of active management. This is logical, since all active managers have access to the same information when competing against one another for possible excess returns. It is therefore very difficult for an active manager to gain and retain a competitive advantage over his or her similarly qualified peers. For every buyer there is an equally well-informed seller, and both think they are making the correct decision. Benjamin Graham described the situation best many years ago when he said, "The stock market resembles a huge laundry in which institutions take in large blocks of each other's washing."[21]

NONFUND INVESTING BY INDIVIDUALS

If active investment management and actively managed mutual funds offer no advantage over passive index funds, then how have individual investors done on their own? According to the 2014 "Quantitative Analysis of Investor Behavior," issued annually by Dalbar, Inc., a Boston-based analytical firm, the average U.S. equity investor achieved an annualized return of 5.02% over the past 20 years, which is 4.2% less than the 9.22% average annualized return of the S&P 500 Index. Over the bull market of the past three years, the average U.S. equity investor gained 10.87% annually, which lagged the 16.18% annual return of the S&P 500 Index by 5.31%.

The average fixed-income investor had an annualized return of only 0.71%, which is 5.03% less than 5.74% return of the Barclays U.S. Aggregate Bond Index over the past 20 years. Both equity and fixed-income investors underperformed their markets over the past 1, 3, 5, 10, and 20 years.

We already know that much of this underperformance is due to investors making poor timing decisions due to their emotional responses to the markets. Investors sell after extended losses and are out when the market rises. Let us look now at some other studies so we can understand more about individual investor behavior.

Using data of 60,000 individual investors at a U.S. discount broker from 1991 through 1996, Goetzmann and Kumar (2008) found that investors are underdiversified. They hold portfolios that are highly volatile and stocks that are highly correlated. This increased volatility can aggravate investors' poor timing decisions.

Using the same data, Kumar (2009) discovered that investors prefer to hold underperforming lottery-style stocks that are low-priced and have high volatility or high skewness.[22] The author determined that the typical investor could have improved his or her performance by 2.8% annually if he or she had simply replaced the lottery component of his or her portfolio with the nonlottery component.

Barber and Odean (2000) noted that the net stock market returns earned by average households lagged reasonable benchmarks by economically and statistically significant amounts. Individual investors turn over 80% of their portfolios annually. As we saw in Chapter 4, investors trade too much due to overconfidence and the disposition effect that makes them greedy and fearful at the wrong times. Warren Buffett recommends doing the exact opposite of this: be greedy when others are fearful and fearful when others are greedy.

Weber et al. (2014), using data from an online European discount broker from 1999 through 2011, found that 5,000 individual European investors earned slightly negative risk-adjusted returns. Like their U.S. counterparts, European investors held only a few stocks, and these were often highly correlated. European investors also had a lottery mentality by preferring low-priced stocks with high idiosyncratic volatility or high idiosyncratic skewness. Eliminating some of these investor behaviors could have improved the average investor's annual returns by 4% for underdiversification and by 3% for lottery stock preferences.

Individual investors are also at a disadvantage in terms of information and expertise. When Michael Steinhardt, the renowned hedge fund manager, was asked what the most important thing an average investor could learn from him, he replied, "I'm their competition."

Warren Buffett said, "Investing is simple but not easy." In summary, individual investors tend to

- Respond overemotionally to market volatility

- Hold high-volatility, lottery-style stocks and underdiversified portfolios

- Be overconfident and overtrade their stock holdings

- Be at an informational disadvantage

Given these tendencies, it would seem best for most investors to adopt instead a disciplined, rules-based approach, such as the one featured in this book.

BLOWIN' IN THE WIND

Studies show that momentum works well with almost any asset class.[23] However, we can maximize our return through intelligent asset choice. Risk premium can serve as a tailwind to accentuate return and ensure that the odds of continuing success remain in one's favor. U.S. stocks, with their 6.7% real return over the past 200 years, represent a strong and forceful wind that can fill the sails of our momentum model. Bonds, with a real return of 3.8%, are like a gentle breeze. Non-U.S. equities, with a risk premium somewhere between these two, are a steady zephyr. Commodities, hedge funds, private equity, and active investment management represent eddies, crosswinds, and head winds that may impede, rather than assist, our forward progress.

Today's overemphasis on diversification often leads to mediocrity and unnecessary expense. (Alternative assets comprise 10% of pension fund assets but earn 40% of total fees paid.) Without discrimination, diversification can become "deworsification." We shall see in later chapters that low-cost equity and fixed-income index funds, appropriately selected by dual momentum, are all that one needs for investment success. As Mae West once said, "Too much of a good thing can be . . . wonderful."

CHAPTER 6

SMART BETA AND OTHER URBAN LEGENDS

Things are seldom what they seem. Skim milk masquerades as cream.

—Gilbert and Sullivan

W E HAVE SEEN WHY WE want to focus on stocks and, to a lesser extent, bonds in our application of dual momentum. (If you do not understand that yet, please reread Chapter 5.) The question then arises, are there better ways to participate in stocks than through traditional capitalization weighted indexes?

Smart beta is a catchall term for rules-based strategies that do not use conventional stock market index capitalization weights. According to Russell Investments, smart beta "includes transparent, rules-based strategies that are designed to provide exposure to market segments, factors, or concepts." Smart beta attempts to deliver a better risk and return trade-off by using alternative weighting schemes based on measures such as volatility, dividends, and market risk factors. Among the best-known alternatives to capitalization weightings are the fundamentally weighted indexes developed in 2005 by Research Affiliates, a leader in the field of smart beta. It ranks stocks by sales, earnings, book value, and cash flow. Dimensional Fund Advisors came out at the same time with its similar Core Equity strategies based on fundamentally based weighting factors. Smart beta also includes equal-weighted funds in place of capitalization-weighted ones.

The global financial crisis of 2007–2008 that led to more interest in diversification and risk control was also an impetus toward smart beta strategies. Interest in smart beta has recently skyrocketed. According to State Street Advisors, smart beta ETFs attracted $46 billion in 2013 and over $80 billion during the preceding three years. Bloomberg reported $156 billion in smart beta products as of February 2014.

Smart beta is the fastest growing segment of the ETF space and grew at an impressive 43% pace in 2013, based on the combined assets under management of the top six managers. Four out of ten (excluding actively managed, leveraged, and inverse) U.S. equities ETFs are now smart beta funds. Institutional investors allocated three times as many assets to smart beta strategies in 2013 as they did the previous year. A Cogent Research study released in January 2014 indicated that one in four institutional investors now use smart beta ETFs, and nearly half of those not currently using them say they are likely to start using them within the next three years.

The first problem with smart beta is that, like unicorns, there is no such thing. Since beta is simply a portfolio's sensitivity to movements in the overall market, it cannot be smart or dumb, although those who use it certainly can be. The expression *smart beta* makes as much sense as *smart correlation*, *smart standard deviation*, or *smart Justin Bieber*. Morningstar has now sensibly renamed smart beta as "strategic beta."[1]

SMART BETA CHARACTERISTICS

Amenc, Goltz, and Le Sourd (2009) and Perold (2007) show that fundamental indexation (a form of smart beta) is actually an active management strategy with a value tilt that is not necessarily superior to capitalization weighting. Chow et al. (2011) show that any apparent outperformance of alternative beta strategies over capitalization-based indexes is due to their exposure to value and small-cap factors.

Research Affiliates acknowledges that the value premium does indeed explain much of its indexes' performance. Figure 6.1 is a price chart of the PowerShares FTSE RAFI US 1000 (PRF) ETF, based on the largest 1,000 fundamentally ranked companies by Research Affiliates, and the iShares Russell

Figure 6.1   PowerShares FTSE RAFI 1000 and iShares Russell Mid-Cap Value

Mid-Cap Value (IWS) ETF from the time when PRF was launched in late 2005. Performance of PRF and IWS has been very similar, with IWS coming out a little ahead.[2] IWS has an annual expense ratio of 0.25%, versus 0.39% for PRF. Some other passively managed ETFs with factor tilts have annual expense ratios of only 0.07% to 0.12%. Smart beta investors in PRF are paying an additional fee for the construction of an index that is very similar to a traditional mid-cap value index. Other smart beta ETFs similarly match up well with lower-cost value and small-cap/mid-cap ETFs.

Looking now at equal-weighted indexing, the average market cap of the S&P 500 Index is about $58 billion, while the average market cap of the S&P 500 Equal Weight Index is only around $16 billion. The S&P 500 Index contains a substantially larger number of relatively smaller-cap stocks than larger-cap ones. Due to its equal dollar weighting, a much larger portion of the total dollars invested in the S&P Equal Weight portfolio is invested in these smaller-cap stocks. Figure 6.2 shows the Guggenheim S&P 500 Equal Weight (RSP) ETF matched up with the iShares Russell 2000 (IWM) small-cap ETF, starting

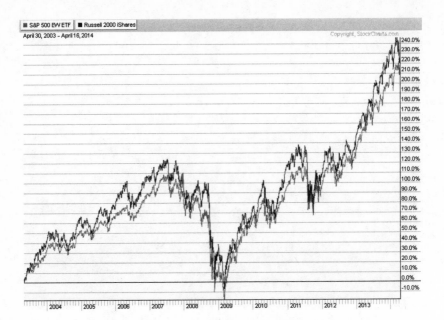

Figure 6.2   Guggenheim S&P 500 Equal Weight and iShares Russell 2000

in 1999 when RSP began. IWM outperforms RSP, which may be due largely to its annual expense ratio of 0.20%, versus 0.40% for RSP, and its lower annual portfolio turnover ratio of 19% versus 37%.

Figure 6.3 shows the capital market line with the return and risk plotted for the S&P 500 Index, the S&P 500 Equal Weight Index, and the U.S. stock market separated into Center for Research in Security Prices (CRSP) size deciles. CRSP 1-2 is large cap, CRSP 3-5 is mid cap, and CRSP 6-10 is small cap. Annual return is on the vertical axis, while annual standard deviation is on the horizontal axis. We see that the S&P 500 Equal Weight Index lies between mid and small cap in its reward-to-risk profile, and that it offers a reward commensurate with its level of risk. Instead of paying a premium for the S&P 500 Equal Weight Index fund, investors could instead just buy a small- to mid-cap index fund.

In addition, the weightings of equal-weight portfolios move continuously away from their target levels, which requires frequent rebalancing and

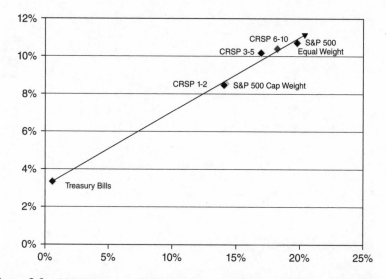

Figure 6.3   S&P Indexes and CRSP Deciles Return Versus Volatility, 1990–2012

substantially higher transaction costs. Frequent rebalancing also involves selling recent winners and buying recent losers, which goes against the momentum effect.

Back in the early 1970s, some of the early adopters of passive investing chose equal-weighted portfolios but gave up on that idea because of the issues of higher turnover, higher volatility, and having to invest large amounts in illiquid stocks.

Low volatility/minimum variance portfolios also suffer from very high portfolio turnover costs. Using data from 1967 through 2000, Hsu, Kaleshik, and Li (2012) replicated smart beta strategies as closely as possible using conventionally available products. Here are their annual portfolio turnover figures: S&P 500 Indexing 6.7%, Fundamental Indexing 14%, Equal Weight Indexing 22.9%, and Minimum Variance Indexing 49.2%. Low volatility/ minimum variance can also have high tracking error, which measures how much a strategy return differs from its benchmark return. While low volatility and low beta strategies show some promise in academic tests, the problems of implementation with respect to portfolio turnover and tracking error may eliminate much of their advantage.

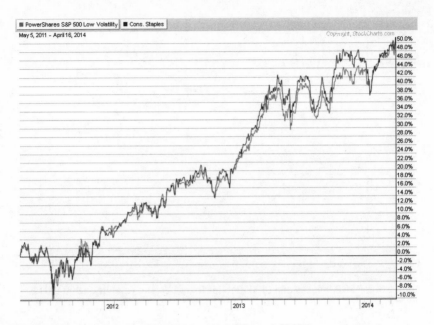

Figure 6.4   PowerShares S&P 500 Low Volatility and SPDR Consumer Staples Select Sector

Sector concentration can be another problem for low volatility strategies. The S&P 500 Low Volatility Index invests in the 100 stocks of the S&P 500 Index having the lowest volatility over the preceding 12 months. It does not constrain sector weights, which can result in huge sector concentrations that cause large tracking errors. Right now, for example, 62% of the S&P Low Volatility Index is in three sectors, and 76% is in four sectors. There have been times in which over two-thirds of the index has been in only two sectors. Figure 6.4 shows how well PowerShares S&P 500 Low Volatility (SPLV), based on the S&P Low Volatility Index, matches up with just the defensive, low volatility SPDR Consumer Staples (XLP) sector.

HOW TO REPLICATE SMART BETA

Here is a way you can replicate a smart beta ETF with a lower-cost, factor-based ETF. Go to the Morningstar online home page, input the symbol of your smart beta ETF in the Quote box, click on the word *Quote*, then look down the page and click on the Portfolio tab in the menu row that begins with the word *Quote*. You will then see the most appropriate benchmark portfolio for that ETF.[3] You can then search online for an appropriate ETF representing that benchmark. For comparison purposes, you can also find annual portfolio turnover ratios and annual expense ratios by clicking on the Morningstar Fees & Expenses tab.

Here is an example using PDP, which is the PowerShares DWA Momentum Portfolio managed by Dorsey, Wright & Associates. This fund uses relative strength momentum applied to individual stocks. The appropriate benchmark for it, according to Morningstar, is the Russell Midcap Growth Index.

Figure 6.5 shows how the PowerShares DWA Momentum Portfolio (PDP) matches up with iShares Russell Mid-Cap Growth (IWP). IWP has a lower annual expense ratio of 0.25% versus 0.67% for PDP, and a lower annual portfolio turnover of 25% versus 66%.

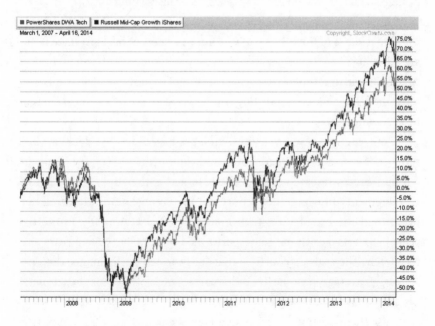

Figure 6.5   PowerShares DWA Momentum Portfolio and iShares Russell Mid-Cap Growth

SMARTER WAYS TO USE SMART BETA

William Sharpe and Eugene Fama have called smart beta (or fundamental indexing) a marketing ploy.[4] George "Gus" Sauter, former chief investment officer at Vanguard Group, said, "These so-called smart betas are not by definition adding alpha; they're merely delivering factor exposures in more costly ways."

Is there any reason then to use smart beta when you can often replicate it at a lower cost? The answer is an unqualified . . . maybe. There are some strategies, such as dividend appreciation, insider sentiment, spin-offs, buybacks, and high quality that may offer more than just factor tilts and sector concentration. While smart beta strategies are more expensive than passive strategies, they are also less expensive than active strategies since there is less day-to-day decision making involved. Another reason to consider smart beta strategies is that passive, capitalization-weighted indexes are not completely efficient.[5] Nor are they optimal, given that prices are noisy (having unpredictable and nonrepeatable patterns) and do not fully reflect all available information.

However, when looking at smart beta strategies, one needs to keep in mind that some of them have only around 15 years of backtest history and are still unproven. Investors with Wayback Machines, who can go back in time to invest, may find these useful. The rest of us, however, will want to see more data than that. Extrapolating results based on only 15 years of data can be very dangerous.

Constructing new, smart beta indexes based on past data can be a futile endeavor. Dickson, Padmawar, and Hammer (2012) of The Vanguard Group issued a research report called "Joined at the Hip: ETF and Index Development," in which they report that the average new index fund outperformed the broad U.S. stock market by 10.3% annually in the five years before its launch but underperformed by 1.0% in the five years after its launch. The authors conclude that "back tested performance does not appear, on average, past the live index date . . . possibly because benchmarks are often chosen for new products based on their attractive past history."

I use the following criteria when I construct dual momentum portfolios to determine if a nontraditional smart beta strategy might be worth considering as a substitute for a capitalization-weighted index and is more than just a high-cost, factor-based closet index fund:

1. Does the approach make logical sense? Are there concepts underlying the strategy that have proven themselves? How likely is it that the strategy will continue to give better than market risk-adjusted returns?

2. Does the approach hold up under rigorous backtesting? Does it show robustness by being consistent across multiple markets and/or different periods?

3. Anomalies often show a decrease in profitability over time due to increases in trading activity.[6] Are strategy transaction costs and fund expense ratios low enough so the approach can hold up to possible declining gross profits?

4. Is volatility of the strategy within a reasonable range? The marketplace may not compensate high volatility. High volatility may also contribute to greater tracking error.

5. Is there decent liquidity in whatever investment vehicles are available for this strategy?

Once an appropriate strategy is found, one needs to review it on a regular basis. What makes sense now may no longer make sense a year or two from now. Rather than deal with all this complexity and uncertainty, for most investors, simply using traditional capitalization-weighted indexes is most likely a better approach. In support of this, West and Larson (2014) of Research Affiliates wrote that smart beta earns around 2% more than market-cap indexes, and it is not the weighting method but rebalancing that creates most of that excess return. Booth and Fama (1992) showed in general that mean reversion rebalancing leads to annual profits of 2% over benchmark portfolios. Smart beta investors may therefore be able to capture the same incremental returns from just a rebalanced stock/bond or sector portfolio.

DOES SIZE REALLY MATTER?

Because many smart beta strategies attempt to pick up size and/or value premia, it might be useful to see how strong the size and value premia themselves really are. A number of researchers have shown that the small-size premium has largely disappeared since at least the 1980s.[7] Shumway and Warther (1997) concluded the small-cap anomaly was likely driven by a mistake in how researchers treated missing data for delisted stocks, which were mostly small caps. Highly illiquid, difficult-to-trade microcaps drive whatever size effect that might still exist. This suggests that the small-size premium may actually be compensation for liquidity risk.

Small-size stocks have more liquidity than they used to, however, because of the proliferation of funds that jumped on the small-cap bandwagon. In 1981, Dimensional Fund Advisors (DFA) dedicated its first stock fund to small-cap equities. It did this shortly after Rolf Banz published a paper based on his University of Chicago PhD dissertation that identified a small-cap premium from 1936 through 1975. DFA soon had several small-cap funds to take advantage of this perceived anomaly. Many other small-cap funds followed soon thereafter.

Increased participation in small caps may explain why the small-size premium has become statistically insignificant since the early 1980s. For example, from December 1978 through 2013, the Russell 2000 Index generated an annualized return (12.1%) almost identical to the larger-cap Russell 1000 and S&P 500 Indexes (12.0%). Small-cap stocks actually underperformed their large-cap counterparts in Europe and Asia from July 1990 through 2013.

Small caps often are inconsistent performers, having underperformed large caps for decades at a time, such as during the 1950s and 1980s. Israel and Moskowitz (2013) recently completed the most current analysis of the size premium. Using 86 years of U.S. stock data from July 1926 through December 2011, they found no evidence of a significant small-size premium over the entire sample, or over any of the four 20-year subperiods. Small size no longer offers abnormal risk-adjusted profits except in illiquid microcaps. Since microcap stocks are more costly and difficult to trade, most investors, particularly institutional ones, avoid this area of the market. Small-cap stocks may add some diversity to a large-cap portfolio, but they also add considerable volatility and nothing in the way of abnormal returns.

DOES VALUE REALLY MATTER?

Since the 1992 Fama and French seminal paper "The Cross-Section of Expected Stock Returns," investors have believed that a significant value premium exists and that it can give value-oriented investors an edge. There are now hundreds, if not thousands, of investment programs and funds incorporating a tilt toward value stocks.

The Israel and Moskowitz (2013) paper thoroughly addressed the value premium issue as well as the size premium issue. They based their findings on the standard book-to-market equity ratio and similar simple indicators of the value premium. More sophisticated value-oriented approaches, such as the one by Gray and Carlisle (2013), may give different results.

Working with the most common indicator of value, the book-to-market ratio, Israel and Moskowitz find the value premium to be insignificant in the two largest quintiles of stocks. These represent the largest 40% of NYSE stocks and are the stocks that are large enough for institutional investor portfolios to include in their portfolios.

Only the smallest-size stocks show a significant value premium. The two smallest quintiles contain stocks that are much smaller than the small-cap Russell 2000 Index. There is no reliable value premium among large-cap stocks in three out of four subperiods from 1927 through 2011. The two largest-size quintiles exhibit a significant value premium only from 1970 through 1989.

The 1992 and 1993 Fama and French studies that started all the excitement about value investing and were the impetus for so many value-oriented funds and portfolios covered a similar 1963–1991 period. This may have just been a unique 28-year period where value stocks produced much higher returns. Dual momentum investors can take comfort in the fact that momentum has worked well across nearly all types of equities and all the way back to the year 1801!

Not long after publication of the Fama and French papers, Kothari, Shanken, and Sloan (1995) did their own study showing that the Fama and French findings were subject to possible sample selection bias. Using a different data source, Kothari et al. found no evidence of a significant positive relationship between the book-to-market equity ratio and average returns. Going up against the highly respected Fama and French, the Kothari et al. study attracted little attention then or now.

John Maynard Keynes reportedly once said, "When the facts change, I change my mind. What do you do?" Unfortunately, not many of us are so impervious to confirmation, conservatism, and anchoring biases. Like the falling from grace of the efficient market hypothesis, it may take many years before the academic and professional investment communities fully reevaluate the existence of a value premium. Fama and French (2014) have now updated their earlier work by issuing a new working paper called, "A Five-Factor Asset Pricing Model," in which the combination of profitability (profits divided by book value) and investment intensity (yearly growth in total assets) can replace value as a risk factor.[8]

Value may or may not be a robust driver of abnormal returns, but there is little doubt that momentum is the king of all market anomalies. Meanwhile, followers of smart beta would do well to look for more than just small-cap and value biases in choosing their investment strategies.

DOES MOMENTUM REALLY MATTER?

Israel and Moskowitz (2013) also included cross-sectional stock momentum in their analysis using a 12-month look-back period while skipping the last month. They found that the momentum premium is present and stable across all size groups. The momentum effect is also positive and statistically significant in every 20-year subperiod. There has been no diminution in its effect during the most current 20-year period. Reliable alphas have ranged from 8.9% to 10.3% per year over the four subperiods before transaction costs.

According to Israel and Moskowitz, across all 86 years, cumulative long-only momentum excess returns averaged 13.6% annually, with a standard deviation of 21.8 and a Sharpe ratio of 0.62. Value excess returns averaged 12.4%, with a standard deviation of 26.5 and a Sharpe ratio of 0.47. Small-size excess returns averaged 11.5%, with a standard deviation of 26.3 and a Sharpe ratio of 0.44.[9] Momentum may not only be the "premier anomaly," as per Fama and French (2008). It may be the only true and lasting anomaly.

CHAPTER 7

MEASURING AND MANAGING RISK

This is worse than divorce. I have lost half my money and still have
a wife.

—*Anonymous (obviously)*

OVER THE PAST 30 YEARS ending in 2013, the S&P 500 had an
annual total return of 11.1%, while the average stock mutual fund
investor earned only 3.69%.[1] Around 1.4% of this underperformance was
due to mutual fund expenses. Investors making poor timing decisions
accounted for much of the remaining 6% of annual underperformance. This
is a remarkable amount of underperformance. Bond fund investors also suffered substantially from poor timing decisions. Investors in passively managed index funds have also been subject to behavioral performance gaps.
The Vanguard S&P 500 Index Fund had a 15-year average annual return of
4.58%, while the average investor in that fund earned only 2.68% annually.

There is a strong propensity for investors to buy near market highs and
sell near market bottoms due to what John Maynard Keynes called "animal
spirits." Others have called it fear and greed. The greater the volatility, the
more pronounced the effect.

CGM Focus (CGMFX) was the highest-return stock fund from 2000
through 2010. It had an average annual return of 18.2%, according to
Morningstar, beating its closest rival by 3.4%. During the same time, the
fund's typical shareholder lost 10%! Investors, motivated by greed and fear,

added heavily to the fund near the top and bailed out as the fund neared its bottom. They poured $2.6 billion into the fund in 2007 when it was up over 80%. In 2008, when the fund was down 48%, investors redeemed over $750 million. This is an example of what investors are up against due to their behavioral biases. Remember what Pogo said: "We have met the enemy, and he is us." We need an approach with a modest level of volatility that will not induce emotional responses that take us out of our investments at the most inopportune times.

Daniel Kahneman (2011) pointed out, "Many individual investors lose consistently by trading, an achievement that a dart-throwing monkey could not match." A disciplined, quantitative approach to investing can reduce the influence of "animal spirits" and help provide consistent results.

We should have a good understanding of relative strength momentum from what we learned in Chapter 2. We saw how relative strength momentum gives investors a disciplined framework to work with. Large market losses, however, can still cause investors to overreact and do foolish things. This can be a problem when using relative momentum, since relative strength does little to reduce downside exposure. Relative momentum may even increase downside volatility. Absolute momentum can help overcome this obstacle, so it is important that we understand it well before moving forward.

UNDERSTANDING ABSOLUTE MOMENTUM

Relative strength compares an asset to its peers in order to predict future performance. In academic research, relative momentum is often the same as cross-sectional momentum, which involves sectioning a universe of individual assets into equal segments and comparing the performance of the strongest segments ("winners") to the performance of the weakest ("losers"). Often testing is done on a market-neutral basis by simultaneously buying "winners" and selling short "losers."

Momentum, however, also works well on an absolute or longitudinal basis, in which an asset's own past predicts its future. Moskowitz, Ooi, and Pedersen (2012) decided to call this time-series momentum. In statistics, longitudinal is usually the counterpart to cross-sectional data analysis and would be a more suitable name than time-series momentum, since time series (prices) are the underlying basis for *all* momentum, not just this particular kind of momentum.

I prefer to call what we have here absolute momentum because practitioners are used to hearing about relative and absolute returns. They measure relative returns against other assets or a benchmark, while absolute returns are those returns with respect to just an asset itself. Relative and absolute momentum follows the same logic.

In absolute momentum, we look at an asset's excess return (its return less the return on Treasury bills) over a given look-back period. If the excess return is above zero, then the asset has positive absolute momentum. If the excess return is below zero, then the asset has negative absolute momentum. Absolute momentum is roughly the same as relative momentum applied to an asset paired up with Treasury bills. In simpler terms, absolute momentum asks if an asset has been going up or going down over the look-back period. If it has been going up, then its absolute momentum is positive. If the asset has been going down, then it has negative absolute momentum. Absolute momentum is a bet on the continuing serial correlation of returns, or, in cowboy terms, absolute momentum says, "A horse is easiest to ride in the direction it's already going."

It is possible for an asset to have positive relative momentum if it is strong relative to its peers and to have negative absolute momentum if its own trend has been down. It can also have positive absolute momentum if its trend has been positive and negative relative momentum if another asset has been going up more.

CHARACTERISTICS OF ABSOLUTE MOMENTUM
According to the renowned trend-following trader Ed Seykota:

> Life itself is based on trends. Birds start south for the winter and keep going. Companies track trends and alter their products accordingly. Tiny protozoa move in trends along chemical and luminescent gradients.[2]

Absolute momentum is quintessential trend following.[3] The goal of trend following is to adhere to Warren Buffett's first rule of investing—do not lose money. His second rule is never to forget the first rule. Some well-known discretionary momentum investors of the past, such as Gerald Tsai, quickly went from hero to zero when they were unable to determine a change in market direction. In today's environment of high investment volatility (HIV), those who are investment active should use some form of protection and always practice safe investing.

Trend-following methods, in general, have slowly achieved some recognition and acceptance in the academic community. It is for many (but not all), no longer considered "voodoo finance."[4] A number of researchers have found evidence of profitability and modest predictive power when using trend-following methods and technical analysis signals to forecast future returns.[5] A recent paper by Lemperiere et al. (2014) called "Two Centuries of Trend Following," identified highly significant anomalous excess returns based on an exponentially weighted moving average strategy applied to four asset classes (stock indexes, commodities, currencies, and bonds) across seven countries. Results were stable across both time and asset class, extending all the way back to 1800 for stock indexes and commodities.

In a sense, all momentum is trend following. Relative strength momentum looks at the trend of one asset compared to another, while absolute momentum looks at the trend of an asset with respect to its own past. Both forms of momentum do essentially the same thing: identify price strength that is likely to persist.

While researchers have thoroughly scrutinized relative momentum over the past 20 years, they have ignored trend-following absolute momentum, for the most part, until just recently. This is unfortunate, since absolute momentum often provides better results and has more flexibility than relative momentum. You can apply absolute momentum to a single asset, whereas you need two or more assets to use relative momentum. With relative momentum, you are always eliminating assets from your portfolio in order to use the strongest ones. Absolute momentum lets you hold on to all your assets, as long as their trends remain positive. Absolute momentum therefore gives greater diversification than relative momentum, which can in turn lower a portfolio's short-run volatility. The biggest advantage of absolute momentum over relative momentum, however, is its ability to reduce dramatically portfolio downside vulnerability by exiting positions early during bear markets. Absolute momentum helps one to follow the maxim of the great trader Paul Tudor Jones: "The most important rule in trading is: play great defense, not great offense."[6]

In 2010, I began to explore absolute momentum by comparing risky asset returns to the returns from short- and intermediate-term bonds.[7] Shorter-term bonds are usually stronger than stocks when stocks are trending down. Selecting bonds over stocks during such times is a way of using absolute momentum.

Absolute momentum got a big boost in 2012 from Moskowitz et al. According to their published research, absolute momentum profits were "remarkably consistent across different asset classes and markets." The authors found that a 12-month look-back period had the highest statistical significance from among a range of 1 to 48 months when used with a one-month holding period. Absolute momentum profits were positive for every one of the 58 assets that they examined. Across all markets, the authors found that absolute momentum gave an annual Sharpe ratio greater than 1, which was roughly 2.5 times the nonmomentum Sharpe ratio of these same markets. There was little correlation with passive benchmarks in each asset class or to the standard asset pricing factors. Returns were largest when stock market returns were the most extreme, which means absolute momentum can function as a hedge to extreme events. This also means absolute momentum can serve as a low-cost alternative to expensive hedging programs that try to reduce downside portfolio exposure.

According to Hurst, Ooi, and Pedersen (2012), absolute momentum is just as robust and universal as relative momentum. In their research, absolute momentum performed well in extreme market environments and across 59 markets covering four asset classes (commodities, equity indexes, bond markets, and currency pairs). The authors showed that absolute momentum has been consistently profitable all the way back to the year 1903. After simulated transaction costs and pro-forma hedge fund fees (2% of annual assets plus 20% of profits), absolute momentum achieved a Sharpe ratio of 1, just like the Moskowitz et al. (2012) study. Absolute momentum monthly correlations to both the S&P 500 and U.S. 10-year Treasuries were only –0.05 over the entire period from 1903 to 2011.

In 2012, I was first-place winner of the Wagner Awards given annually by the National Association of Active Investment Managers (NAAIM) for Advances in Active Investment Management. The paper I submitted was "Risk Premia Harvesting Through Dual Momentum." Half of dual momentum is absolute momentum. In that paper, I demonstrated how absolute momentum gave better long-run results than relative momentum. Not only did absolute momentum offer higher expected returns but, unlike relative momentum, it also substantially reduced downside exposure during bear markets.

In 2013, I wrote "Absolute Momentum: A Universal Trend-Following Overlay." This paper demonstrated the usefulness of absolute momentum as a trend-following overlay, as well as a stand-alone strategy, under different scenarios. I also explored look-back periods and confirmed the value of using a 12-month period with absolute momentum. I demonstrated how absolute momentum can improve risk parity portfolios by reducing their exposure to bonds and their need for leverage. I have included that paper as Appendix B of this book.

Low volatility portfolios have recently become popular owing to their somewhat favorable past performance relative to the broad market indices. The reason for their attractive relative performance primarily is due to their lower volatility in down markets. Absolute momentum can provide greater downside protection than low volatility portfolios while preserving more upside market potential. It can also do this without the tracking error, sector concentration, and high turnover issues associated with low volatility portfolios, as identified in Chapter 6.

DUAL MOMENTUM—THE BEST OF BOTH WORLDS

Even though absolute momentum often gives better risk-adjusted results than relative momentum, most practitioners use only relative momentum. Absolute momentum is still relatively unknown and has not yet attracted much attention.

The best approach is to use absolute and relative together in order to gain the advantages of both. The way we do that is by first using relative momentum to select the best-performing asset over the preceding 12 months. We then apply absolute momentum as a trend-following filter by seeing if the excess return of our selected asset has been positive or negative over the preceding year. If it has been positive, that means its trend is up and we proceed to use that asset. If our asset's excess return over the past year has been negative, then its trend is down and we invest instead in short- to intermediate-term fixed-income instruments until the trend turns positive. This way, we are always in harmony with the trend of the market. Go market!

ALPHA AND SHARPE RATIO

Before we move on to actual model development, we need to assemble a group of quantitative tools to help us evaluate our strategies and make informed decisions about them. Academics often use factor pricing model alphas to evaluate the efficacy of trading strategies relative to appropriate benchmarks. Advantages of this approach are that you can use risk factors that are most appropriate to the model you are testing, and results can be evaluated using standard tests of statistical significance. The biggest drawback to this approach is that it ignores downside exposure, also known as drawdown. Alpha may be useful to look at in terms of ascertaining statistical significance, but we need to use other measures in order to evaluate strategy risk.

A common measure that considers risk in the form of volatility is the Sharpe ratio. The Sharpe ratio is closely related to the t-statistic used for measuring the statistical significance of differential returns. The Sharpe ratio divides an asset's excess average return (return less the risk-free rate) by the standard deviation of that return.[8] It is a measure of the efficiency of a strategy that tells you how much return you earn per unit of risk that you bear. A higher Sharpe ratio indicates a better risk-adjusted return. A Sharpe ratio of 1.0 or greater is very good. For example, Ilmanen (2011) reports a typical Sharpe ratio of 0 to 0.5 for a single asset using a trend-following strategy, which rises to 0.5 to 1.0 when looking at a portfolio of assets.

There are some potential problems, however, with the statistical properties of the Sharpe ratio. For example, rankings based on Sharpe ratios can be misleading if they are not adjusted for the impact of serial correlation. Researchers also usually compare differences in Sharpe ratios, which, due to the additive nature of variance error, is not as accurate as comparing Sharpe ratios of differences. Furthermore, the Sharpe ratio makes no distinction between upside and downside volatility. It penalizes equally both downside risk and upside return potential. Some researchers supplement their use of the Sharpe ratio with the Sortino ratio that uses only volatility below the mean. The Sortino ratio, however, discards all information on upside volatility and the right tail of the distribution, which may be useful to identify profit opportunities.[9] For our internal work, we prefer to use a skewness-adjusted Sharpe ratio, which is easy to calculate and provides additional useful information.[10] For our purposes here though, we will use the standard Sharpe ratio, since others are more familiar with it.[11]

TAIL RISK AND MAXIMUM DRAWDOWN

For normal distributions, upside and downside volatility are approximately the same, but financial market returns are usually non-normally distributed. The difference between upside and downside volatility can be particularly problematic when returns are highly skewed, or nonsymmetric. Stock market returns are often negatively skewed, with an asymmetric left tail extending more toward negative values.[12] This creates tail risk, which can lead to greater-than-expected losses and aggravate the animal spirits mentioned earlier. Positive skewness is much preferred, since surprises should then work in our favor.

Academic research often just ignores tail risk. However, left tail risk, indicating negative skewness, is undesirable from a practitioner point of view. It can lead to large equity erosions, emotional distress, and untimely investor withdrawals.[13] What we need is an indicator of maximum adverse consequences so we can avoid strategies that have too much left tail risk.

One such indicator is conditional value-at-risk (CVaR), also known as expected shortfall. CVaR uses the actual distribution of returns to determine the expected loss of a portfolio when there is a loss. CVaR is difficult to calculate, and the results are not intuitively appealing. I find it difficult to relate to the CVaR values and prefer instead to use a visual indicator called a box plot. This shows on one comparative chart median returns, interquartile ranges of returns, and expected extreme values.

Another simple indicator of tail risk that is intuitive, easy to understand, and relatively easy to calculate is maximum drawdown.[14] Drawdown is the percentage that price moves down from a new high. Since we use monthly returns, maximum drawdown to us means the maximum cumulative peak-to-valley retracement on a month-end basis.[15]

As with most things, there are some potential drawbacks to using maximum drawdown. First, maximum drawdown is dependent on the length of one's performance record. All else being equal, maximum drawdown increases with track-record length. Therefore, it is most useful when maximum drawdown is used to evaluate strategies having the same amount of performance history and plenty of historical data. Second, maximum drawdown represents only a single occurrence. The number of drawdowns that occur and drawdowns other than the very worst one may also be important to us. To get a better sense of the depth, quantity, and duration of drawdowns, I look at drawdowns in different ways, at different times, and under different conditions.

AN INTEGRATED APPROACH

We are now ready to evaluate our strategies numerically and visually using comparative returns, standard deviations, profit consistency, alphas, Sharpe ratios, box plots, and maximum drawdowns under different scenarios.

We have looked at the history and evolution of momentum, the rationales that support it, and what we should or should not include as investment assets. Now that we have the requisite background information and some useful evaluation tools, we can move on to model development and presentation. In the next chapter, we will put all the pieces together and see what dual momentum can really do for us.

CHAPTER 8

GLOBAL EQUITIES MOMENTUM

> There is a tide in the affairs of men which, when taken at the flood, leads to fortune.
>
> *—William Shakespeare*

WE HAVE SEEN HOW MOMENTUM evolved, what assets are best to include in a momentum-based model, and what we mean by relative, absolute, and dual momentum. We have also identified the tools and criteria we need for evaluating our results. We are ready now to create an integrated model that transforms momentum concepts into a real-world experience.

Based on the past success and high-risk premium of equities, we will anchor our investment portfolio in U.S. stocks and switch into non-U.S. stocks in accordance with relative strength momentum. We will hold bonds (short to intermediate term) only when the U.S. and non-U.S. equity markets are not in an uptrend, as determined by absolute momentum. This should minimize any drag that a bond allocation might have on the long-run performance of our strategy, while allowing bonds to come into play and contribute fully to portfolio returns during equity bear markets.

DYNAMIC ASSET ALLOCATION

Our dual momentum approach using both absolute and relative momentum to manage asset allocation is a major paradigm shift from what investors usually have done. Typically, investors have a permanent allocation to diversifying assets, such as bonds, since they do not have a way to exit equities early on in bear markets.

Greater integration of world markets now and higher intermarket correlations are other reasons that permanent asset allocations may not make as much sense as they once did. Converging asset correlations under market stress means that permanent diversification may not provide the risk reduction that investors want. For example, when U.S. and non-U.S. equities enjoy returns that are one standard deviation above average, which is typical of bull markets, their monthly correlation is –0.17. However, when equity returns are one standard deviation below average, which is typical of bear markets, the monthly correlation between U.S and non-U.S. equities rises to 0.76. Dual momentum can take us from naive diversification to a dynamically adaptive asset allocation approach that keeps us better in tune with changing market regimes and less exposed to converging market correlations.

LOOK-BACK PERIOD

The momentum formation or look-back period is the amount of history we use to measure momentum and select our momentum-based portfolio. We saw earlier that the best look-back period across most markets is generally 6 to 12 months.

The majority of academic literature covering both relative and absolute momentum agrees that a 12-month look-back period gives the best performance. A number of commercial momentum applications also use a 12-month look-back period.[1] We will similarly use a 12-month look-back period and apply it to both types of momentum. Other look-back periods also deliver satisfactory results. However, a look-back period at the long end of the 6- to 12-month effective range minimizes portfolio turnover and transaction costs.

In dealing with individual stocks, one often skips the most recent week or month in order to disentangle the intermediate momentum effect from the short-term reversal or contrarian effect in returns at the one-week or one-month level. This is said to be related to liquidity or microstructure issues. We will use broad-based stock market indexes for our momentum model, because they are less subject to noise than individual stocks, and their transaction costs are much lower. Indexes are also less subject to liquidity and microstructure issues, so we will not need to skip a month.

APPLIED ABSOLUTE MOMENTUM

We will first look at absolute momentum applied to the S&P 500 Index. This means if the S&P 500 shows a positive excess return (return less the Treasury bill return) during the past 12 months, we stay invested in it. If the prior 12-month excess return of the S&P 500 is negative, we exit the S&P 500 Index and hold the Barclays U.S. Aggregate Bond Index instead. We stay in aggregate bonds until the excess return of the S&P 500 is again positive. The Barclays U.S. Aggregate Bond Index is a relatively stable index of high-quality, investment-grade (78% AAA-rated) bonds with an average maturity under five years.[2] Since its inception in 1976, it has held up well during every bear market in stocks. This should make it a relatively safe place to park our capital when the stock market is weak.[3] What we are doing in effect is staying in stocks if the market has been up for the past year and exiting to the safety of shorter-term bonds if the stock market has been down for the past year. Our approach is both simple and easy.

Table 8.1 and Figure 8.1 show the results of applying absolute momentum to the S&P 500 Index versus the S&P Index without the application of absolute momentum.[4]

Because absolute momentum takes us out of the S&P 500 and into aggregate bonds 30% of the time, we also show the results of a passive benchmark portfolio that is always invested 70% in the S&P 500 and 30% in aggregate bonds.

Something as simple as the application of 12-month absolute momentum gives impressive results. Average annual return increases by more than 200 basis points over the S&P 500 Index by itself, while the annual standard

Table 8.1   S&P 500 Absolute Momentum, 1974–2013

	Annual Return	Annual Std Dev	Annual Sharpe	Maximum Drawdown	% Profit Months
S&P 500 Index	12.34	15.59	0.42	–50.95	62
Aggregate bond	7.99	5.58	0.46	–12.74	69
S&P 500 + aggregate bond*	11.01	11.45	0.47	–37.62	64
S&P 500 absolute momentum	14.38	12.23	0.69	–29.58	66

* 70% S&P 500 and 30% aggregate bond

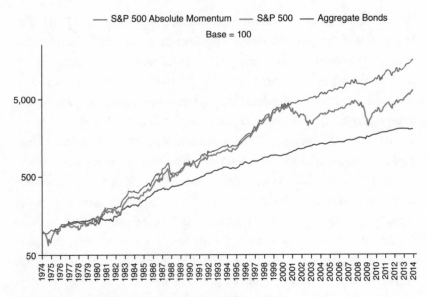

Figure 8.1   S&P 500 Absolute Momentum, 1974–2013

deviation drops by more than 3%. Maximum drawdown goes from over 50% to less than 30%. Figure 8.1 shows graphically how absolute momentum sidesteps severe bear market drawdowns, as it did in both 2000 and 2008, while capturing most of the markets upside gains. This is another chart you should stare at until the message fully sinks in.

Being a long-term trend-following approach, absolute momentum will not respond to short-term market corrections such as the one that occurred in October 1987. That may be a good thing, since sharp corrections like that often create oversold conditions followed by quick market rebounds. Long-term market tops usually take some time to form as the markets transition from a state of accumulation to a state of distribution. Market technicians look for patterns such as double tops or head-and-shoulder formations to identify such transitional states.

As you can see from Figure 8.1, absolute momentum, being trend following in nature, was not able to exit at the exact market tops in 1981, 1989, 2000, or 2007. However, absolute momentum gave back relatively little in accumulated profits before exiting stocks. It would have taken us out of harm's way early during each bear market.

During bull markets, absolute momentum usually stays dormant, acting as a form of stop loss. However, unlike an actual stop loss, absolute momentum has an inherent way to reenter the market once the trend turns positive again.

Professional money managers would gladly give up their firstborn for long-term results that are as good as the absolute momentum results shown in Table 8.1. We can clearly see how effective absolute momentum is when applied to the U.S. stock market. All stock market investors and professional money managers would do well to take notice of absolute momentum.

APPLIED RELATIVE MOMENTUM

In order to use relative strength momentum, we need to have two or more assets to choose from. The MSCI All Country World Index (MSCI ACWI) is a float-adjusted, capitalization-weighted index of 24 developed markets and 21 emerging markets. U.S. stocks make up 45% of the MSCI ACWI, other developed markets make up another 45%, and emerging markets comprise the remaining 10%. We will use the MSCI World Index (MSCI World) prior to when the MSCI ACWI became available in January 1988. MSCI World does not include emerging markets. MSCI did not track these until the start of the MSCI ACWI in 1988. From now on, when we refer to ACWI, we mean MSCI ACWI from 1988 onward and MSCI World prior to 1988. We will separate our ACWI into two roughly equal parts: the S&P 500 Index for U.S. stocks and the ACWI ex-U.S. for the rest of the world.

Table 8.2   ACWI, ACWI ex-U.S., and S&P 500, 1974–2013

	Annual Return	Annual Std Dev	Annual Sharpe	Maximum Drawdown	% Profit Months
ACWI	11.52	15.56	0.36	−60.21	61
ACWI ex-U.S.	11.92	17.65	0.34	−64.10	60
S&P 500	12.34	15.59	0.42	−50.95	62

Table 8.2 shows the 40-year performance of the ACWI, ACWI ex-U.S., and the S&P 500 from 1974 through 2013. We see that non-U.S. stocks (ACWI ex-U.S.) and the index of both U.S. and non-U.S. stocks (ACWI) have a significantly lower return than just U.S. stocks. This is in line with what we know about the higher long-run risk premium of the U.S. stock market.

We will next apply relative strength momentum to the S&P 500 and ACWI ex-U.S. components of the ACWI. (Results are nearly identical using a broader based index for U.S. stocks, such as the Russell 3000 or the MSCI US Broad Market Index.) We use the large-cap S&P 500 to be consistent with the types of stocks selected in the non-U.S. portion of the ACWI.

RELATIVE VERSUS ABSOLUTE MOMENTUM

Each month we can apply absolute momentum to ACWI by switching between it and the Barclays U.S. Aggregate Bond Index based on whether the excess return of the S&P 500 has been positive or negative during the past 12 months. We use the S&P 500 to determine the trend of all our equities indexes, because the United States leads world equity markets, according to Rapach, Strauss, and Zhou (2013). We apply relative momentum to ACWI by selecting the stronger of its two components based on their relative performance over the preceding 12 months. Table 8.3 and Figure 8.2 show the results of both relative and absolute momentum applied to the ACWI and its components, versus the performance of the ACWI index itself without the use of momentum.

We see that relative strength momentum applied to ACWI gives a 289 basis point greater annual return than ACWI itself. This comes with

Table 8.3   MSCI All Country World Index and Momentum, 1974–2013

	Annual Return	Annual Std Dev	Annual Sharpe	Maximum Drawdown	% Profit, Months
ACWI	11.52	15.56	0.36	−60.21	61
Relative momentum	14.41	16.20	0.52	−53.06	63
Absolute momentum	12.66	11.93	0.57	−23.76	66

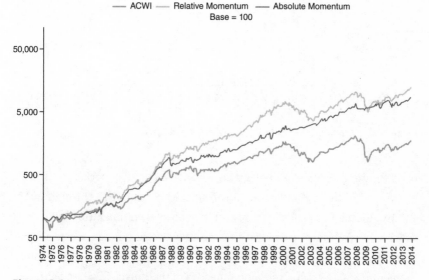

Figure 8.2   ACWI with Relative and Absolute Momentum, 1974–2013

a slight increase in volatility and a modest reduction in maximum draw-down. Absolute momentum gives a more modest 114 basis point increase in return over ACWI, *but with a 3.6% decrease in standard deviation and more than a 60% reduction in maximum drawdown.* Absolute momentum is particularly helpful in bear market environments, such in 2000–2002 and 2007–2008.

Figure 8.3 shows the ratios of the cumulative returns of relative and absolute momentum to the ACWI index. We see here how well relative and absolute momentum complement each other. Absolute momentum kicks in and adds value in bear market years, such as 1982, 2001, and 2008. Relative momentum, on the other hand, adds value during those times when absolute

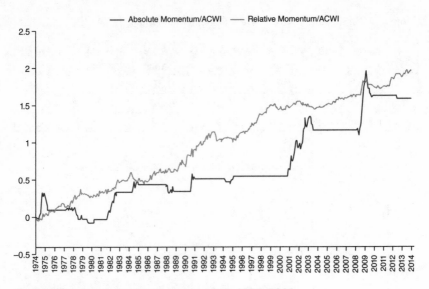

Figure 8.3   Cumulative Growth Versus ACWI, 1974–2013

momentum is dormant and offers no advantage over the market itself, such as from 1986 through 2000, 2003 through 2007, and 2011 through 2013. Relative momentum adds more return than absolute momentum, but it does so with considerably more volatility and drawdown. It is also worth noting that the correlation between the monthly returns of relative and absolute momentum is 0.69, which supports the idea of their diversification value.

Investors currently use relative momentum much more than they use absolute momentum. Absolute momentum, though, with its substantial decrease in volatility and drawdown and its higher Sharpe ratio, is superior on a risk-adjusted basis. We are not limited, however, to using just one of these types of momentum. We can benefit from the complementary nature of relative and absolute momentum by using them both together. This is what dual momentum is all about.

APPLIED DUAL MOMENTUM

Let us see now what happens when we combine absolute and relative momentum together in order to form dual momentum. Aggregate bonds will again serve as a safe harbor during bear markets in accordance with our absolute momentum signals taken from the S&P 500. We will also switch between the S&P 500 and the ACWI ex-U.S. based on relative strength momentum. My name for this particular application of dual momentum is Global Equities Momentum (GEM). It truly is a gem. Figure 8.4 illustrates the logic behind GEM.

We first compare the S&P 500 to the ACWI ex-U.S. over the past year and select whichever one has performed better. We then check to see if our selected index has done better than U.S. Treasury bills. If it has, we invest in that index. If it has not, we invest instead in U.S. aggregate bonds. We repeat this procedure every month.

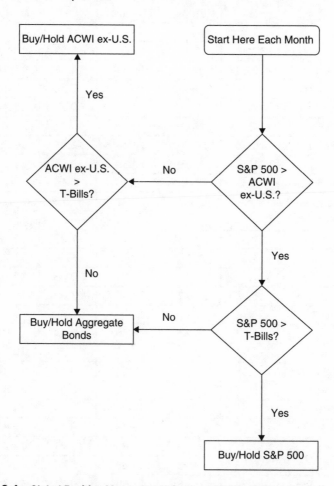

Figure 8.4   Global Equities Momentum Using Last 12-Month Total Returns

From 1974 through October 2013, GEM spent 41% of its time in the S&P 500, 29% in the ACWI ex-U.S., and 30% in aggregate bonds. There were only 1.35 switches per year on average between these three assets, which means transaction costs for index switching would have been negligible.[5] Table 8.4 shows the performance of ACWI dual momentum (GEM), ACWI relative momentum, ACWI absolute momentum, and benchmarks of the ACWI index and a permanent 70/30% split between ACWI and U.S. aggregate bonds.

Table 8.4   Momentum Performance by Decade, 1974–2013

	GEM	Relative Momentum	Absolute Momentum	ACWI	ACWI+AGG*
All Data					
Annual return	17.43	14.41	12.66	11.52	10.45
Annual std dev	12.64	16.20	11.93	15.56	11.37
Annual Sharpe	0.87	0.52	0.57	0.36	0.41
Max drawdown	−17.84	−53.06	−23.76	−60.21	−45.74
1974–1983					
Annual return	15.95	15.41	12.46	11.44	10.53
Annual std dev	11.77	16.39	10.83	13.95	11.04
Annual Sharpe	0.54	0.36	0.30	0.16	0.13
Max drawdown	−10.95	−32.77	−11.91	−32.78	−25.37
1984–1993					
Annual return	22.39	20.58	16.03	17.27	15.66
Annual std dev	14.60	16.68	13.54	15.66	11.45
Annual Sharpe	0.97	0.75	0.64	0.63	0.74
Max drawdown	−15.78	−22.72	−23.76	−27.02	−18.56
1994–2003					
Annual return	17.87	10.73	12.46	8.34	7.94
Annual std dev	12.21	16.11	11.45	15.22	10.66
Annual Sharpe	1.02	0.38	0.67	0.26	0.34
Max drawdown	−15.37	−48.85	−16.43	−56.52	−33.32
2004–2013					
Annual return	13.68	11.69	9.78	9.22	7.82
Annual std dev	11.83	15.68	11.85	17.31	12.27
Annual Sharpe	0.96	0.58	0.53	0.43	0.50
Max drawdown	−17.84	−53.06	−21.69	−60.21	−45.74

*70% ACWI and 30% aggregate bond

Over this entire 40-year period, GEM has an average annual return of 17.43% with a 12.64% standard deviation, a 0.87 Sharpe ratio, and a maximum drawdown of 17.8%.[6] This almost doubling of the annual rate of return over ACWI comes with a reduction in volatility of 2%. The Sharpe ratio quadruples, and the maximum drawdown drops by nearly two-thirds.

As you can see in Figure 8.5, the absolute momentum component in GEM kept us relatively safe from bear market erosions of capital.[7] Not having to recoup bear market losses is what contributed greatly to GEM's extraordinary returns. As an indication of robustness, GEM also showed consistency throughout the data, having much higher Sharpe ratios and lower maximum drawdowns than ACWI during each of the four decades.

Figure 8.6 is a reward-to-volatility plot for GEM, absolute momentum, relative momentum, and the ACWI index. It is easy here to see that GEM has the best reward-to-risk profile.

Figure 8.7 shows 12-month rolling returns of GEM and ACWI. It gives an indication of extreme upside and downside annual returns. GEM is more consistent in earning positive returns, and it has fewer extreme downside excursions. GEM was weak relative to ACWI in the early 1980s due to the highly unusual situation of short-term interest rates rising to 20%, making Treasury bills temporarily more attractive than equities. GEM was also weaker than ACWI in early 1975, late 2002, and early 2009 when ACWI

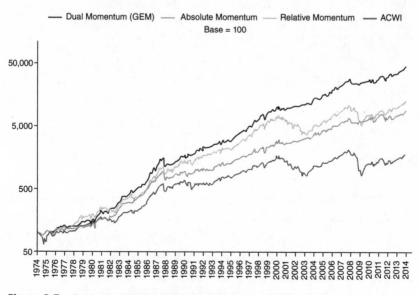

Figure 8.5   Dual, Absolute, and Relative Momentum, 1974–2013

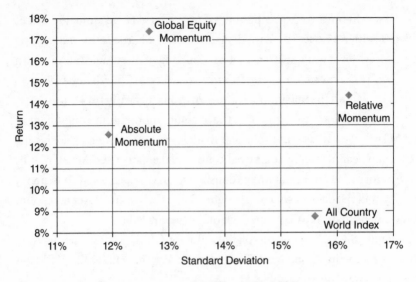

Figure 8.6   Portfolio Return Versus Volatility, 1974–2013

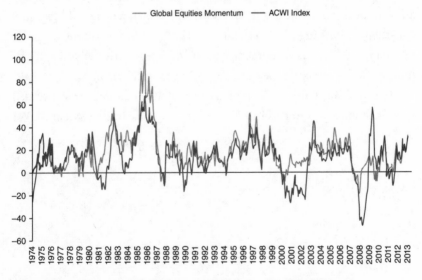

Figure 8.7   GEM and ACWI Rolling 12-Month Returns, 1974–2013

rebounded sharply following large bear market losses. Otherwise, GEM consistently outperformed ACWI.

As a check on robustness, Table 8.5 shows GEM with look-back values ranging from 3 to 12 months. All GEM look-back configurations are superior to ACWI in terms of Sharpe ratio and maximum drawdown.

Table 8.5   GEM Look-Back Periods, 1974–2013

	GEM12	GEM 9	GEM 6	GEM 3	ACWI
Annual return	17.43	15.85	14.37	13.90	8.85
Annual std dev	12.64	12.39	11.84	12.04	15.56
Annual Sharpe	0.87	0.78	0.71	0.65	0.22
Max drawdown	−17.84	−18.98	−23.51	−23.26	−60.21

Figure 8.8 shows the cumulative performance of GEM, relative momentum, and absolute momentum in relation to ACWI. Notice how much stronger dual momentum is than either absolute or relative momentum. We also
see how GEM benefited from absolute momentum in 1982, 2001, and 2009,
when relative momentum offered no advantage over the market. On the
other hand, GEM benefited most from relative momentum in 1986 through
1998 and 2004 through 2007 when stocks were strong and absolute momentum provided no advantage over the market. This again illustrates how one
can use absolute and relative momentum together in an effective and complementary way.

GEM was much stronger than ACWI in 1974, 2001, and 2008 when
ACWI suffered through three severe bear markets. This contrary performance

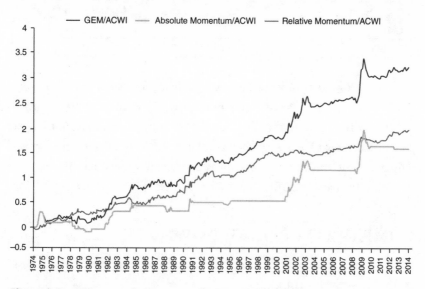

Figure 8.8   Differences in Cumulative Growth, 1974–2013

during bear markets shows that GEM could have a valuable place as a stabilizing and diversifying asset for those equity investors who do not want to use GEM as a core holding.

GEM investors should keep in mind that GEM does not necessarily outperform the market on a short-term basis. This is especially true when the market is rebounding sharply from deeply oversold bear market conditions, as we saw in Figure 8.7. Trend following typically lags behind market action. The long-term net effect, however, is very positive for GEM.

To get a better sense of how and when GEM achieves its outperformance, Table 8.6 shows the number of years that GEM outperformed and underperformed the S&P 500 during up and down years for the S&P 500. Table 8.7 shows average annual returns in those up and down market environments.

Table 8.6   Years of Outperformance, 1974–2013

	S&P 500 Up Years	S&P 500 Down Years
GEM > S&P 500	14	8
S&P 500 > GEM	13	0
GEM = S&P 500	5	0

Table 8.7   Average Annual Returns, 1974–2013

	S&P 500 Up Years	S&P 500 Down Years
GEM	21.9	2.2
S&P 500	18.5	–15.2

GEM's low-risk profile makes it less likely that investors will make emotionally based exit decisions at inopportune times when other equity investors are rushing toward the sidelines. GEM investors still need to exercise patience during bull markets when GEM may just as often underperform as outperform market benchmarks. Investors need to remember that much of the outperformance of GEM occurs in bear market environments.

COMPARATIVE DRAWDOWNS

Table 8.8 shows the amounts, lengths, and recovery times of the five largest GEM and ACWI drawdowns.

Table 8.8   Five Largest GEM and ACWI Drawdowns, 1974–2013

Drawdown Amount	Start Date	Low Date	Recovery Date	Peak to Trough Months	Trough to Recovery Months	Peak to Recovery Months
GEM						
−17.84	9/87	10/87	5/89	1	19	20
−17.49	11/07	10/08	12/10	11	24	35
−16.1	5/11	9/11	2/12	4	5	9
−15.4	7/98	8/98	11/98	1	3	4
−8.6	4/00	7/00	7/01	3	12	15
ACWI						
−53.9	11/07	2/09	?	16	>46	>62
−50.5	3/00	3/03	10/06	30	49	79
−30.8	3/74	9/74	3/76	7	18	25
−27.0	12/89	9/90	12/93	9	48	57
−20.4	8/87	11/87	1/89	3	14	17

Figures 8.9 through 8.12 offer different views of GEM drawdowns and returns compared to those of ACWI and other benchmarks.

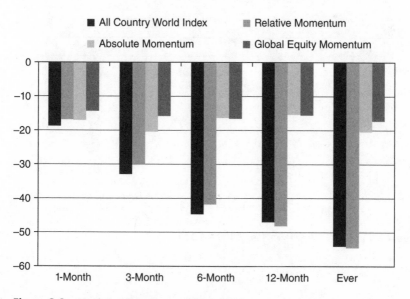

Figure 8.9   Maximum Drawdowns, 1974–2013

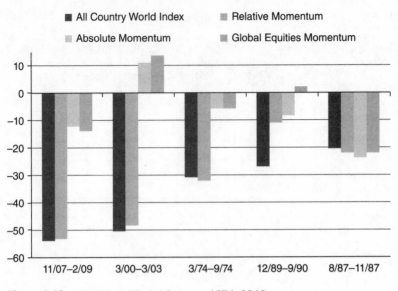

Figure 8.10   ACWI Bear Market Returns, 1974–2013

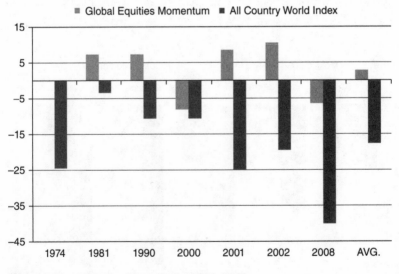

Figure 8.11   ACWI Drawdown Years, 1974–2013

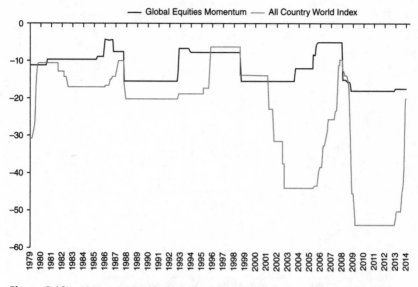

Figure 8.12   GEM and ACWI Rolling Five-Year Maximum Drawdown, 1979–2013

Figure 8.13 shows GEM quarterly returns plotted against corresponding ACWI quarterly returns rolling forward through the data one month at a time. We see in the lower left quadrant of the chart how the

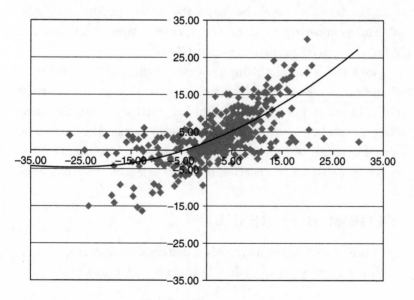

Figure 8.13   Quarterly Returns GEM versus ACWI, 1974–2013

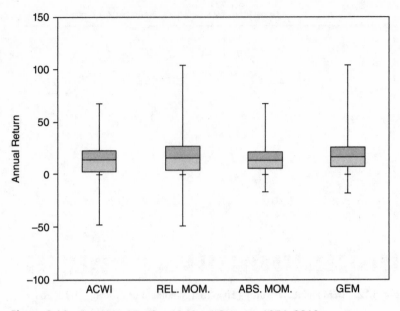

Figure 8.14   Box Plot of Rolling 12-Month Returns, 1974–2013

use of absolute momentum in GEM truncates much of the drawdown that shows up in ACWI. On the other hand, the upward sloping linear relationship in the upper-right quadrant of the chart shows that most positive ACWI returns pass through unaltered to GEM.

Figure 8.14 is a box plot giving a reward-to-risk view based on rolling 12-month returns. Box plots give a simultaneous view of each strategy's reward and variability characteristics. The long vertical lines are the ranges of returns (excluding extreme outliers), while the rectangular boxes show interquartile ranges bounding 50% of the returns. Each model's median 12-month return is the horizontal line that splits its box into different colors.

FACTOR MODEL RESULTS

Using multiple regression factor models as described in Chapter 3, Table 8.9 shows GEM returns regressed against the Fama-French-Carhart four-factor

Table 8.9   Factor Pricing Models, 1974–2013

	Alpha*	Market	Size	Value	Momentum	Bond	R²
Five-factor model	5.30 (2.67)	0.50 (8.32)	–0.06 (1.10)	0.08 (1.32)	0.20 (4.25)	0.37 (3.50)	0.44
Four-factor model	5.94 (2.99)	0.53 (9.64)	–0.09 (1.83)	0.09 (1.43)	0.21 (4.39)	–	0.44
Three-factor model	5.80 (3.25)	0.47 (8.29)	–	–	0.17 (5.00)	0.39 (3.88)	0.43

*Alpha is annualized. Newey-West robust t-statistics are in parentheses.

market, size, value, and momentum risk factors as per the Kenneth French website data library.[8] Since the GEM model is in bonds around 30% of the time, we also show a five-factor model that adds the excess return of the Barclays Aggregate Bond index as an additional factor. In addition, we show a simple three-factor model using only stock market, bond market, and momentum risk factors.

Under all three of these factor models, GEM provides economically and statistically significant risk-adjusted excess returns (alpha). Since GEM is long only, we naturally see highly significant coefficients on the stock and bond market factors. GEM also has a highly significant loading on stock momentum, showing that relative strength momentum plays a significant role in the strong performance of GEM.

SIMPLE AND EFFECTIVE

GEM is not only effective in providing high and significant risk-adjusted returns, but it is also parsimonious. This is a word used by economists to make them look smart. It means simple and straightforward. Einstein once said, "Everything should be kept as simple as possible, but no simpler." In the words of Antoine de Saint-Exupéry, "Perfection is achieved not when there is nothing more to add, but when there is nothing left to take away," and in the words of Mr. Rogers, "Deep and simple is far more essential than shallow and complex."

Highly optimized methods are often complex, fragile, and prone to failure. GEM, on the other hand, is simple and robust. It uses only U.S. equities, non-U.S. equities, and aggregate bonds. Its only parameter is a 12-month look-back period validated in hundreds of in- and out-of-sample momentum studies across many diverse markets and over two centuries of market data. These in- and out-of-sample results and the simplicity and robustness of GEM minimize any data mining and overfitting bias, the usual banes of model construction.

HOW TO USE IT

GEM is simple to implement using exchange-traded funds (ETFs), which have lower operating expenses, more trading liquidity, more transparency, and more efficient tax structures than mutual funds.[9] One can easily determine GEM rebalancing signals using an online charting program. I suggest PerfCharts by StockCharts.com,[10] because it uses total returns, whereas most other free charting programs use only price changes in their chart construction. You need to enter and save three ETF symbols, one each for U.S. stocks (IVV, or VOO), non-U.S. stocks (VEU or VXUS), and U.S. Treasury bills (BIL). Each month you plot the performance of these three ETFs over the past 253 trading days (one calendar year). If one of the two equity ETFs shows the highest return over the past year, then that is your selection for the coming month. If U.S. Treasury bills show the highest return, this means the stock market trend has been down, and you hold an aggregate bond ETF instead (AGG, BND, or SCHZ).

The costs associated with implementing and managing GEM should be extremely low. There are commission-free ETFs at four different brokerage firms one can use to implement the GEM strategy: Vanguard, Charles Schwab, TD Ameritrade, and Fidelity Investments. The average annual expense ratio of Vanguard's S&P 500, FTSE All-World ex-U.S., and U.S. Total Bond ETFs is only 10 basis points.[11] GEM is also relatively tax efficient. Dual momentum usually sells losing positions, creating short-term capital losses while holding onto winning positions for long-term capital gains. Can there be any reason not to use GEM?

ACCOMMODATING DIFFERENT RISK PREFERENCES

We will see in the next chapter that there is little or nothing gained from adding complexity to GEM. Being so simple, one might wonder if there is any way for GEM to match the varying risk profiles of different investors.

To answer that, we use the Markowitz-Tobin fund separation theorem, which separates the decision of what assets to hold from the decision of how much risk to assume.[12] More specifically, this says that investors should hold the singular portfolio of assets having the highest Sharpe ratio, but those wanting a lower-risk profile should combine that optimal portfolio with a risk-free (or low-risk) alternative asset. Conversely, aggressive investors wanting higher returns can borrow in order to leverage the optimal portfolio.

Figure 8.15 shows the separation theorems tangency portfolio, where a straight line (the capital market line) originating from the risk-free rate just touches the efficient frontier of risky portfolios. Risk-averse investors will have a better reward-to-risk ratio and will be better off investing along this line rather than on the efficient frontier itself.

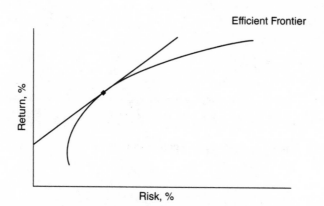

Figure 8.15   Capital Market Line and the Efficient Portfolio Set

Table 8.10 and Figure 8.16 show GEM leveraged 30% to suit aggressive investors who choose to borrow at the federal funds rate plus 25 basis points. It also shows GEM combined with a 30% permanent weighting to aggregate bonds in order to create a more conservative portfolio for more risk-averse investors. GEM can, in this way, be a program for all seasons and for many different investors.

Table 8.10   Global Equities Momentum, Leveraged and Deleveraged

	Ann. Return	Annual Std Dev	Annual Sharpe	Maximum Drawdown	% Profit, Months
GEM 130	20.13	16.43	0.81	−23.37	65
GEM	17.43	12.64	0.87	−17.84	68
GEM 70	14.52	9.50	0.90	−12.13	69

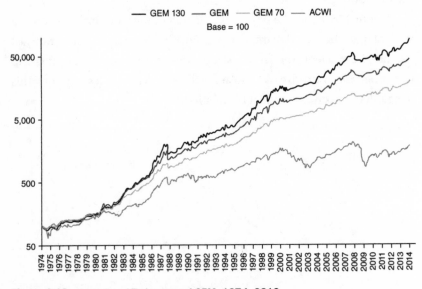

Figure 8.16   Leveraged/Deleveraged GEM, 1974–2013

CHAPTER 9

MO' BETTER MOMENTUM

Simplicity is the ultimate sophistication.

—Leonardo da Vinci

W E SAW IN THE LAST chapter how dual momentum gives us higher expected returns with lower expected risk. Chapters 5 and 6 looked at other investment approaches and reinforced why dual momentum is what we should focus on. We saw, in particular, that the propensity to overdiversify is counterproductive to those who understand and are smart enough to implement dual momentum strategies. What we want to look at now are some possible ways to enhance dual momentum and some additional ways we might use it.

DANGERS IN TRYING TO ENHANCE MOMENTUM

Dual momentum is simple and direct, based as it is on straightforward relative and absolute performance. Its main parameter is the look-back period. Cowles and Jones first discovered abnormal profits from relative strength momentum in the U.S. stock market with a 12-month look-back using data from 1920 through 1935. Many other researchers have confirmed this approach in other markets and with additional data up to the present and all the way back to 1903 with absolute momentum and 1801 with relative momentum. With so many years of out-of-sample validation, we should not have to worry about data-snooping bias. The fact that a 12-month look-back works well with both forms of momentum serves as a cross-validation of 12 months as a good length for our look-back period.

With so much going for dual momentum, if you try to replace or modify this proven approach with something new, you face several potential problems. First is the multiple-comparisons hazard that comes from data mining when it becomes data snooping. If you look at enough different strategies, almost certainly a few of them will look attractive. However, this simply can be due to chance or luck. If you measure statistical significance at the 5% level, for example, and you test 20 or more strategies, you will likely end up with one that appears significant when it is not, since it can still occur 1 in 20 times by chance alone. One does not need to experiment extensively to get into trouble this way. In an aptly named study called "Pseudo-Mathematics and Financial Charlatanism: The Effects of Backtest Overfitting on Out-of-Sample Performance," Bailey et al. (2014) state, "high performance is easily achievable after backtesting a relatively small number of alternative strategy configurations. . . . [I]nvestors can be easily misled into allocating capital to strategies that appear to be mathematically sound."

There are some infamous examples of what can happen when you rely only on data snooping to develop an explanatory model. Around 20 years ago, two researchers found they could explain 99% of the return on the S&P 500 Index using a multiple regression on butter production in Bangladesh, cheese production in the United States, and the number of sheep in the United States and Bangladesh. Those researchers still get inquiries asking where one can find data on Bangladesh butter production! There have been other studies linking stock market returns to the number of nine-year-old children in the United States, the length of women's dress hemlines, and whether or not an American graces the cover of the annual *Sports Illustrated* swimsuit edition.[1]

The same data-snooping problem exists after you choose a model and have to determine its parameters. With momentum, there is only one parameter: the look-back period. By now, researchers have validated it every which way from Sunday. However, most models are not so simple, and there is always the risk of model overfitting and overspecification.

By adding complexity to a model, you may make it too rigid by molding it perfectly to "predict" the past. It may then be ineffective at forecasting the future. According to López de Prado (2013), because financial data exhibits memories of various sorts, overfitting does not just lead to noise (randomness). It often leads to systematic out-of-sample losses due to mean reversion. The better the backtested results, the worse the subsequent real-time results.

There is also the problem of using the data twice, once to optimize a strategy and its parameters, and then again to judge how well the strategy predicts future returns. One needs to penalize complex or highly optimized models and to evaluate performance on fresh data not used for model development. López de Prado goes on to show that standard statistical techniques designed to prevent overfitting, such as splitting data into a development set for testing and a holdout set for cross-validation, can still be inaccurate when used for backtesting purposes. There are a number of reasons for this, the main ones being that the holdout method does not account for the number of attempted trials, and researchers may already know what happens in the second half of the data. As Nobel laureate physicist Richard Feynman pointed out, "if the process of computing the consequences is indefinite, then with a little skill any experimental result can be made to look like the expected consequences."[2]

Besides multiple comparison hazards and overfitting biases, data mining can also suffer from a paucity of data. Some practitioners use only around 15 years of data to design and backtest their trading models, since that is when a number of ETFs started trading. These results are suspect, given the amount of noise there is in financial data. Return distribution parameters are time varying and regime dependent. Relatively short data samples are usually not representative of the whole, and they often do not give repeatable backtest results. The property in which every sequence or sample of data is equally representative of the whole is called ergodicity. Financial markets are most definitely nonergodic. Some stock market regimes may never repeat, while others repeat with considerably different characteristics. The following is one way to see this.

Let us define the variance ratio (VR) as the ratio of the variance of the k-period return to k times the variance of the 1-period return. When returns are uncorrelated over time, the numerator and denominator will be the same, so the VR will be 1. In a mean-reverting market, returns are negatively correlated, and the VR will be less than 1. In a trending market, returns will be positively correlated, and the VR will be greater than 1. If we calculate the VR over various k periods, we will be able to tell if the market has been trending or mean reverting over those periods.

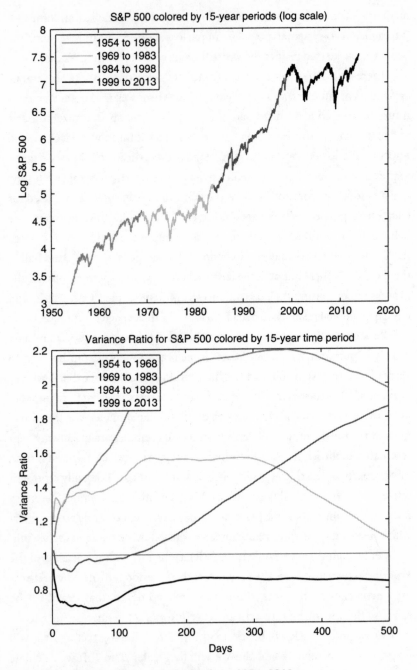

Figure 9.1   Variance Ratios: 15-Year Periods, 1954–2013

Source: Tony Cooper

Tony Cooper provided the charts for Figure 9.1.[3] Figure 9.1*a* shows the S&P 500 identified by 15-year time intervals. Figure 9.1*b* shows the VR associated with each of these 15-year intervals. We see that for the 1999–2013 interval (the lowest line on the VR chart), the market was mean-reverting over all the *k* periods. For other 15-year intervals, the VR values are mostly higher than 1, indicating trending markets. The diverging VR chart patterns show us that backtests performed on only 15 years of data are unlikely to give reliable forward-looking predictions. One of the most frequent mistakes I see others make is using only a limited amount of data, such as 15 years, to develop a model and then expect it to give reliable results going forward in time. The prominent researcher Kenneth French (Fama and French, 2007) once said that 78 years of data in the Center for Research in Security Prices (CRSP) database might not be enough to separate out noise from one's results.[4] We saw in Chapter 6 that respected researchers determined there was a significant value premium based on 28 years of data. Now that substantially more data is available, we see that the value premium, like the size premium before it, might be suspect.

In contrast to this, significant and consistent risk-adjusted profits from absolute momentum go back to 1903. With relative momentum, results extend even farther back, to 1801. As far as I know, there is no other backtesting in financial markets that is based on this much data.

Having plenty of data lets you see how consistent and stable your results are across a wide range of market conditions, and whether or not they depend on just a few periods of short-term outperformance. Worst-case scenarios, in particular, are highly dependent on the amount of past data that is available. The statistician W. Edwards Deming once said, "In God we trust; all others bring data." With these caveats in mind, let us look at some alternative ways of determining price trends that are in keeping with the principles underlying absolute momentum. We will also examine some possible enhancements to relative strength momentum.

ABSOLUTE MOMENTUM REVISITED

There have been many attempts by practitioners over the years to engage in market timing and determine price trends. Before the decade of the 2000s, there was common agreement among most academics that market timing does not work. The statement of Malkiel (1995) was typical at the time: "Technical analysis is anathema to the academic world. We love to pick on it." Just the words "market timing" would shut down most academic's and many practitioner's brain synapses.

After publication of the paper "Simple Technical Trading Rules and the Stochastic Properties of Stock Returns," by Brock et al. in 1992, academic attitudes toward technical analysis and trend-following methods slowly started to change. Brock et al. applied 26 technical trading rules to the Dow Jones Industrial Average (DJIA) from 1897 through 1986. Their study reduced data-snooping bias by reporting all possible results, using a very long data set, and looking for robustness across various subperiods. They were also among the first to extend standard statistical tests using bootstrap techniques. Overall, their results supported the use of technical trading strategies. On the other side of the issue, Fang, Jacobsen, and Qin (2013) found poor out-of-sample performance when they retested the exact same 26 Brock et al. trading rules on 25 years of new data. In their paper "What Do We Know About the Profitability of Technical Analysis?" Park and Irwin (2007) gave a summary of the mixed state of trend-following results. The authors found that among 95 modern studies of technical trading strategies from 1988 through 2004, there were 56 with positive results, 29 with negative results, and 19 with mixed results. The authors concluded that most empirical studies were subject to problems in their testing procedures related to data snooping, ex-post selection of rules, and not accounting properly for risks and transaction costs.

More recently, Bajgrowicz and Scaillet (2012) applied 7,846 trading rules to the daily Dow Jones Industrial Average from 1897 through 2011. Using an up-to-date correction for data-snooping bias, the false discovery rate (FDR), the authors found that investors would never have been able to select the best performance rules ahead of time.[5] Introducing transaction costs would have eliminated whatever profits did exist.

Along the same lines, Fang, Qin, and Jacobson (2014) examined the profitability of 93 market indicators (50 market sentiment and 43 market strength indicators) applied to S&P 500 data averaging 54 years in length. After accounting for transaction costs, none of the indicators outperformed buying and holding the S&P 500 on a risk-adjusted basis, and there was no evidence that they showed predictability with respect to future stock returns.

We see that data mining for new trading rules is a perilous undertaking. Although bootstrapping can help establish confidence levels, especially when dealing with modest amounts of data, it may depend on assumptions about how the markets function that may not be realistic. More specifically, accurate time-series bootstrapping and simulation results/depend on data ergodicity and stationarity. Since financial markets are nonstationary and nonergodic with possible price jumps and nonfinite variances, bootstrap simulations may have their own potential problems.

The simplicity and robustness of absolute momentum gives it an edge over unproven and uncertain alternative trend-following methods. With that in mind, let us look cautiously at a few other trend-following approaches that are in keeping with what we know about absolute momentum.

Baltas and Kosowski (2012) came up with an alternative method for determining absolute momentum trends using a broad data set of 75 futures contracts from December 1975 through February 2013. They compared the usual method of determining absolute momentum that looks at the direction of preceding 12-month returns to an alternative method based on the t-statistic of the slope found by fitting a trend line to daily prices over the past 12 months. Their method reduced the transaction costs of absolute momentum by about two-thirds. The authors found that the Sharpe ratios of the two methods were virtually the same before transaction costs, but that commodity and fixed-income contracts came out ahead under their alternative method once transaction costs were included.

TREND FOLLOWING WITH MOVING AVERAGES

Moving averages have been one of the most popular and longstanding methods among practitioners for determining price trends. Gartley (1935) wrote about moving averages in the 1930s. William Gordon (1968) helped popularize the 200-day moving average. Using data from 1897 through

1967, Gordon showed that buying stocks when the DJIA was above its 200-day moving average produced seven times the return as when the DJIA was below its 200-day moving average.

Once a whipping boy for academic researchers, moving averages for market timing has in recent years gained some acceptance and support. Since 2002, Jeremy Siegel of Wharton has presented the 200-day moving average as a volatility-reducing filter in his popular book *Stocks for the Long Run*. Faber (2007) converted the 200-day moving average into an equivalent 10-month moving average, whereby one holds a long position when the price is above its 10-month moving average and exits the position when the price falls below the 10-month moving average. This cuts down on the number of trades and whipsaw losses that occur when using a daily moving average.

Whether we are talking about a 10-month average or 200-day one, the moving average length does raise some data mining concerns. Brock et al. (1992), Siegel (2014), and Faber (2007) all acknowledge that the 10-month/200-day moving average length has historically been the most popular one among practitioners. Prior to these studies, practitioners likely tested many moving average lengths to arrive at this particular one.

Faber's paper "A Quantitative Approach to Tactical Asset Allocation" attracted considerable attention to the 10-month moving average rule. His paper has received the highest number of downloads in its category on the Social Science Research Network (SSRN). It inspired other research papers and a subsequent book by Faber and Richardson (2009). A number of practitioners have adopted this popularized 10-month moving average approach.

We can easily compare the 10-month moving average to our absolute momentum strategy. Table 9.1 shows the results of applying a 10-month moving average, a 12-month moving average (used by other practitioners), and 12-month absolute momentum to the S&P 500 Index from 1974 through 2013. When not invested in stocks, all three strategies are in U.S. aggregate bonds.

Results from the three strategies were very similar. Absolute momentum was in stocks 70% of the time. It had 31 trades over these 40 years, for an average of 0.83 trades per year. The 10-month moving average was in stocks 74% of the time and had 49 trades, or 1.2 trades per year. Absolute momentum

Table 9.1   S&P 500 Absolute Momentum and Moving Averages, 1974–2013

	12-Month Absolute Momentum	10-Month Moving Average	12-Month Moving Average	S&P 500, No Filter
Annual return	14.38	14.16	14.29	12.34
Annual std dev	12.23	12.13	12.23	15.59
Annual Sharpe	0.69	0.68	0.68	0.42
Max drawdown	−29.58	−23.26	−23.26	−50.95

therefore had lower transaction costs than the 10-month moving average. Table 9.1 does not reflect these costs.

Moving averages and absolute momentum both try to identify trends by reducing noise. In 1906, British scientist Sir Francis Galton (cousin of Charles Darwin) first noticed the importance of noise reduction.[6] Galton was attending a fair where 800 people tried to guess the weight of a dead ox. After the prize was awarded, Galton asked if he could see the guesses. Most of them were way off the mark. Galton was shocked, however, to see that the average guess was 1,197 pounds, while the actual weight of the ox was 1,196 pounds! There was a true signal hidden among all the noise. Averaging was able to make sense from apparent randomness.

Absolute momentum reduces noise by looking at two reference points in time. It essentially asks if today's price is higher or lower than the price was 12 months ago. Moving averages reduce noise by smoothing it out through averaging, just as Galton had done.

MARKET TIMING USING VALUATION

Some practitioners believe they can time the market by paying attention to valuation metrics, such as the Shiller 10-year Cyclically Adjusted Price Earnings (CAPE) ratio. CAPE is calculated by taking the S&P 500 and dividing it by the average of 10 years' worth of earnings. The current CAPE ratio is then compared to its long-term average of about 17. Investors look for mean reversion back toward this average. Historically, CAPE ratios under 10 have led to future annual stock market returns of over 20%, while CAPE ratios over 20 have given future annual stock market returns of only 5%.

The current CAPE level of about 26 indicates that the U.S. stock market is expensive compared to historic norms. However, this does not necessarily mean that stocks are near a bull market top. Those who got out of the market in 1996, when the CAPE was at approximately the same level as it is now, would have missed out on seeing the U.S. market more than double in value as the CAPE ratio rose to over 40 in 1999–2000. Paul Tudor Jones noted that the last one-third of a bull market is often the most dramatic, where mania runs wild and prices go parabolic. Market timing based on valuation could miss out on all this.

In addition, the normal level of corporate earnings may have changed over time, and studies of past CAPE levels may have overfit the data. Valuation metrics are only capable of giving a crude approximation of what future returns might be like.[7]

RELATIVE MOMENTUM REVISITED

The majority of momentum studies focus on individual stocks, and most practical applications of relative strength momentum similarly use individual stocks. Because of its popularity, we will also look at applying momentum to individual stocks. Fortunately, the folks at AQR Capital Management LLC maintain readily accessible and freely available momentum-based stock index data on their website.[8]

The AQR Momentum Index is composed of the top one-third of the 1,000 highest capitalization U.S. stocks based on 12-month relative strength momentum with a one-month lag. AQR weights its index positions based on market capitalization. It adjusts its positions quarterly.

Table 9.2 shows the results of the AQR Momentum Index, the Russell 1000 Index, and 12-month absolute momentum (with aggregate bonds as a safe harbor) applied to the Russell 1000 Index from when the AQR momentum indexes began in January 1980.

AQR estimates transaction costs of 0.7% per year for its AQR Momentum Index. These are not accounted for in its index returns or in Table 9.2.

We see that the AQR Momentum Index gave higher returns than the Russell 1000 Index, but that it also had higher volatility over this

Table 9.2   AQR Momentum, Russell 1000, and Absolute Momentum, 1980–2013

	AQR Momentum	Russell 1000	Russell 1000 with Abs Mom
Annual return	15.14	13.09	15.92
Annual std dev	18.27	15.51	12.57
Annual Sharpe	0.49	0.53	0.80
Max drawdown	−51.02	−55.56	−23.41

33-year period. The Sharpe ratios and maximum drawdowns of the two indexes are comparable. Accounting for the 0.7% per year in additional transaction costs for the AQR Momentum Index would have put it at a disadvantage to the Russell 1000 index on a risk-adjusted basis.

The simple addition of absolute momentum to the Russell 1000 Index gives a higher return than the AQR Momentum Index or the Russell 1000 Index, as well as a much lower standard deviation and a greatly reduced maximum drawdown. The absolute momentum Sharpe ratio is also much higher. Transaction costs of using our simple absolute momentum strategy would be negligible, and there would be no fees incurred from managing a large portfolio of individual stocks. There seems little reason to choose an individual stock momentum strategy over using a low-cost, broad-based stock index combined with simple absolute momentum.

In their 2014 working paper "Fact, Fiction, and Momentum Investing," Asness, Frazzini, Israel, and Moskowitz of AQR argue that momentum applied to individual stocks is worthwhile even if it were to show a zero return, provided one combines momentum stocks with value stocks.[9] This is because value and momentum exhibit a pronounced negative correlation.

Table 9.3 shows the AQR Momentum Index, the Russell 1000 Value Index, and a 50/50 combination of momentum and value as used in Asness et al. (2013). We see that value combined with momentum does give a slightly higher Sharpe ratio than either value or momentum alone. However, there is little or no advantage with respect to maximum drawdown, and results still pale in comparison to absolute momentum combined with the Russell 1000 Index.

Table 9.3   AQR Momentum, Russell 1000 Value, 50/50 Momentum, and Value, 1980–2013

	AQR Momentum	Russell 1000 Value	50/50 Momentum and Value	Russell 1000 with Abs Momentum
Annual return	15.14	13.52	14.33	15.92
Annual std dev	18.27	14.87	15.71	12.57
Annual Sharpe	0.49	0.53	0.55	0.80
Max drawdown	–51.02	–55.56	–51.47	–23.41

Furthermore, two of the four authors of Asness et al. (2014), Israel and Moskowitz, are the same authors who showed in their own 2013 paper that value, as it is commonly used, only offers a historic premium when applied to very small stocks, which are generally unusable by institutional investors.

Perhaps we can find other ways to improve upon individual stock momentum so that it becomes more useful. There have been dozens of research papers exploring possible enhancements to relative strength momentum. I will touch on four that look promising for individual stocks. We may also be able to apply two of these enhancements to market indexes or to assets other than stocks. Those who want to explore the potential enhancements in more detail can download the referenced research papers while keeping in mind the caveats given previously about data mining and model overspecification.

PROXIMITY TO 52-WEEK HIGHS

In the 1950s, both Dreyfus and Darvas extolled the virtue of investing in stocks that were making new highs. In their 2004 paper "The 52-Week High and Momentum Investing," George and Hwang showed that the 52-week high explains a large portion of the profits from momentum investing. Using U.S. stocks from 1963 through 2001, the authors calculated the ratio of the current stock price to the 52-week stock price high. They then demonstrated that profits based on nearness to the 52-week high plus the highest returns over the past six months were superior to profits based solely on the highest returns over the past six months. Nearness to the 52-week high dominated the forecasting power of past returns. The authors postulated that stocks near their 52-week high are those for which good news has recently arrived. If this is really the reason why being near a 52-week high is effective, then nearness to a 52-week high is likely to be more effective with individual stocks than with stock indexes or asset classes that may not be as sensitive to news events.

PRICE, EARNINGS, AND REVENUE MOMENTUM

In their 2013 paper, "Does Revenue Momentum Drive or Ride Earnings or Price Momentum?" Chen et al. (2014) examined the profitability of strategies based on price, earnings, and revenue momentum, both alone and in combination with one another. Looking at U.S. stocks from 1974 through 2007, the authors measured price momentum based on past stock returns, as is usually done. They also measured earnings and revenue momentum, which they based on historical earnings and revenue. Using long/short hedged portfolios, the authors found that price momentum gave the largest average profit, followed by earnings, then revenue momentum. None of the three momentum strategies was dominant, which means that each carried some exclusive information content. The authors sorted all three factors into quintiles and matched up the top quintiles of each factor to create a double sort. Hedged portfolios from double sorts on two of the three factors, on average, outperformed single-sort portfolios. The one portfolio formed from a triple sort of all three factors outperformed all the double-sort portfolios. Revenue and earnings momentum combined accounted for only 19% of the price momentum effects, so price momentum was the most important factor. Overall evidence suggests that a strategy combining past return, earnings, and revenue momentum outperforms strategies based on only one or two of these factors. Since this approach incorporates earnings and revenue information, it would apply only to stocks and not to other asset classes.

ACCELERATING MOMENTUM

In their 2013 paper, "Investor Attention, Visual Price Pattern, and Momentum Investing," Chen and Yu investigated visual patterns of past stock prices that indicate momentum acceleration, garner investor attention, induce overreaction, and amplify the momentum effect.

For U.S. stocks from 1962 through 2011, the authors performed a linear regression of daily returns against the square of time in order to determine the price trajectory curvature. A positive coefficient indicated convex price trajectory curvature, whereas a negative coefficient indicated concave curvature.

When the authors sorted stocks based on this curvature, they found that the gross returns and three-factor alphas of convex (accelerating upward) positive momentum stocks were significantly higher than the gross returns and alphas of stocks with concave positive momentum. The authors showed that ignoring positive momentum stocks with concave price trajectories is the key to earning higher momentum returns.

Docherty and Hurst (2014) took a similar approach in the Australian stock market using data from 1992 through 2011. They measured the slope of recent performance relative to the 12-month geometric average rate of return. They called this shorter-term relative performance "trend salience." Doing a double sort on trend salience and traditional momentum, the authors found that the combined approach significantly outperformed traditional momentum. Accelerating momentum as either curvature or trend salience might be effective with stock indexes and other assets, in addition to its use with individual stocks.

FRESH MOMENTUM

In "Fresh Momentum," Chen, Kadan, and Kose (2009) defined fresh winners as the strongest stocks during the previous 12 months that were relatively weak during the 12 months prior to that. Stale winners, on the other hand, are those stocks that were strongest during both periods. Doing a double sort by quintiles on relative price strength in months 1 through 12 (excluding the most recent month) and months 13 through 24 for U.S. stocks from 1926 through 2006, the authors found that fresh winners outperformed stale winners by 0.43% per month. One could easily apply this fresh momentum approach to stock indexes and other assets, in addition to individual stocks.

GLOBAL BALANCED MOMENTUM

Earlier I mentioned that we could use dual momentum in other ways besides our GEM model. The following are two proprietary models I developed that utilize dual momentum.

The simplest extension of dual momentum is to start with the allocation given for conservative investors in Chapter 8 that permanently has 70% in GEM and 30% in U.S. aggregate bonds. This time, instead of holding the permanent fixed-income portion of the portfolio always in U.S. aggregate bonds, we will use dual momentum to select from among the following fixed-income alternatives: Barclays Capital U.S. Long Treasury, Bank of America Merrill Lynch Global Government, Bank of America Merrill Lynch U.S. Cash Pay High Yield, and 90-day U.S. Treasury bills.

I call this dual momentum global stock/bond strategy my Global Balanced Momentum (GBM) model. GBM has 70% allocated to the same equities holdings as GEM, but its fixed-income holdings, including a permanent 30% allocation to fixed income, are selected from the previous list of fixed-income alternatives using dual momentum. This means that the equity portion of the portfolio when stocks are weak, as well as the fixed-income portion, can be in any of the fixed-income alternatives mentioned in the last paragraph, depending on which of them has been the strongest over the look-back period.

GBM has substantial advantages over traditional stock/bond balanced portfolios. Average returns of the typical 60% stock/40% bond portfolio have barely kept pace with inflation across 7 of the 11 decades since 1900. A typical 60/40 balanced stock/bond portfolio had negative real returns over rolling 10-year periods almost one-quarter of the time over the past 114 years. Severe and lengthy drawdowns have also been common, including ones of −66% and −55%.

Table 9.4 and Figure 9.2 show the performance of GBM compared with benchmark allocations of 70% GEM with 30% U.S. Aggregate Bonds, 70% ACWI with 30% U.S. aggregate bonds, and a typical balanced portfolio of 60% S&P 500 and 40% U.S. aggregate bonds. We see that applying dual momentum to the fixed-income side boosts the annual return of the conservative 70% GEM/30% U.S. aggregate bond portfolio by over 150 basis points.

Compared to the traditional 60/40 U.S stock/bond balanced portfolio, GBM has twice the Sharpe ratio and only half the maximum drawdown. GBM has both a higher expected return and a lower-risk profile than a typical stock/bond balanced portfolio. GBM has achieved a substantial reduction in maximum drawdown compared to the 60/40 balanced portfolio without having to resort to more than a 30% permanent allocation to bonds.

Table 9.4   Global Balanced Momentum Versus Benchmarks, 1974–2013

	Global Balanced Momentum	70% GEM, 30% Agg Bonds	70% ACWI, 30% Agg Bonds	60% S&P 500, 40% Agg Bonds
Annual return	16.04	14.52	8.59	10.58
Annual std dev	10.06	9.50	11.37	10.15
Annual Sharpe	0.98	0.90	0.28	0.49
Max drawdown	−16.83	−15.46	−45.74	−32.54

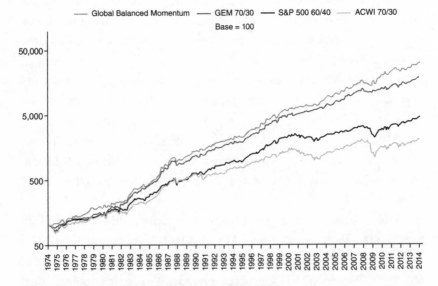

Figure 9.2   Global Balanced Momentum, 1974–2013

DUAL MOMENTUM SECTOR ROTATION

Moskowitz and Grinblatt (1999) postulated that industry components are the primary source of stock momentum profits and that momentum strategies provide compensation for industry risk. They constructed an industry-based momentum strategy that produced the same average monthly returns as an individual stock momentum strategy. Momentum based on industries, or sectors of closely related industries, is much easier to implement than individual stock momentum, and transaction costs are considerably lower.

Another dual momentum strategy is one that rotates among the strongest U.S. stock market equity sectors. The Morningstar sectors separate the U.S. stock market into 11 nonoverlapping segments. These cover technology, industrials, energy, communication services, real estate, financial services, consumer cyclical, basic materials, utilities, consumer defensive, and healthcare.

We can select an equally weighted basket of the top-performing sectors using relative strength momentum in what I call my Dual Momentum Sector Rotation (DMSR) model. When the U.S. stock market is in a downtrend, according to absolute momentum, DMSR moves all of its assets into the Barclays Capital U.S. Aggregate Bond Index. Table 9.5 and Figure 9.3 show how DMSR has performed in comparison to the S&P 500, a portfolio of monthly rebalanced equally weighted equity sectors, and 77% equally

Table 9.5   Dual Momentum Sector Rotation Versus Benchmarks, 1993–2013

	Dual Momentum Sector Rotation	S&P 500	Sector Equal Weight	Equal Weight/ Aggregate Bond*
Annual return	17.93	10.49	11.45	10.17
Annual std dev	12.24	14.91	13.36	10.39
Annual Sharpe	1.13	0.48	0.60	0.66
Max drawdown	−17.21	−50.95	−47.50	−37.83

*77% Equal Weight/23% Aggregate Bond

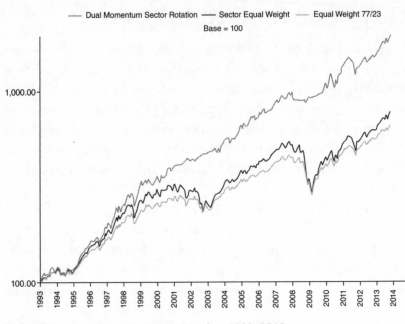

Figure 9.3   Dual Momentum Sector Rotation, 1993–2013

weighted sectors plus 23% U.S. aggregate bonds. We include the last benchmark because DMSR has overall spent 77% of its time in equities and 23% in
U.S. aggregate bonds. Data is from January 1992, which is the starting date of
the Morningstar U.S equity sectors. Monthly rebalancing of sectors captures
some mean reversion profit for all the portfolios other than the S&P 500.[10]

Figure 9.4 shows the contributions to DMSR from both relative and
absolute momentum. We see clearly that absolute momentum offers both
a higher return and a substantially lower drawdown than relative momentum. Dual momentum reflects the higher returns and drawdown reduction
of applying absolute momentum to enter and exit the 11 equally weighted
equity sectors, while also capturing the higher returns that sometimes come
from relative strength momentum. DMSR can also reduce portfolio risk
exposure by rotating into defensive sectors, such as consumer defensive and
utilities, prior to market tops. These defensive sectors often hold up well following market tops and before trend-following absolute momentum can
kick in and take us out of all equity positions.

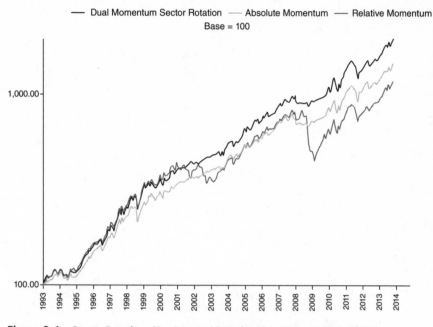

Figure 9.4   Sector Rotation, Absolute and Relative Momentum, 1993–2013

WHAT TO DO NOW

There are many ways to use dual momentum. The risk reduction that comes from absolute momentum frees us to go after markets such as U.S. equities that offer the highest risk premium instead of having to focus on diversification that may not deliver its promised reduction in volatility and drawdown. Although I have developed and use more sophisticated momentum models, the simple GEM model shown in Chapter 8 is a very good model for most investors. It is simple, easy to implement, and not subject to overfitting bias. Readers can find performance updates to my publicly available dual momentum models and answers to frequently asked questions (FAQ) on my website http://www.optimalmomentum.com.

CHAPTER 10

FINAL THOUGHTS

What, me worry?

—Alfred E. Neuman

J OHN MAYNARD KEYNES ONCE SAID, "If economists could manage to get themselves thought of as humble, competent people on a level with dentists, that would be splendid." I do not know what it is about dentists, but Warren Buffett also said, "Full-time professionals in other fields, let's say dentists, bring a lot to the layman. But in aggregate, people get nothing for their money from professional money managers."

Unfortunately, I am too old to attend dental school. As an alternative, I came up with dual momentum. Doing so has been an interesting and rewarding adventure.

Eugene Fama said that the aim of model development is to get you to know more about the markets afterward than when you started. That has certainly been the case for me with respect to dual momentum.

Charles Darwin once wrote, "It is not the strongest of the species that survives, nor the most intelligent, but rather the one most adaptable to change." Dual momentum is nothing if not adaptable. Relative strength momentum goes with the flow in selecting the best-performing assets. Absolute momentum tunes in to market dynamics by adapting to changing market conditions. Adaptation is what ensures our long-run success and ultimate survival.

According to Lao Tzu, the best way to manage anything is by making use of its inherent nature. Dual momentum lets us do that by dynamically

changing our market exposure in accordance with regime shifts while simultaneously exploiting investor behavioral biases and capturing high-relative-
strength returns. One of the ubiquitous sayings of Wall Street is that bull
markets climb a wall of worry. With dual momentum, that expression instead
becomes, "Don't Worry. Be Happy." All we have to do is follow our model.

OLD INVESTMENT PARADIGM

The old investment paradigm starts with naive investing by individual investors, some of whom make decisions by listening to prognosticators. Warren
Buffett commented on this too, saying the only value of stock forecasters is to
make fortunetellers look good. Sturgeon's law also comes to mind: "Ninety
percent of everything is crap." Individual investors often overtrade, underdi-
versify, and succumb to a number of common behavioral errors.

Having others take over the decision-making process through active
investment management usually subjects one to high fees, similar overtrad-
ing, and some of the same behavioral biases that plague individual investors.

The old paradigm also relies on fixed income to reduce portfolio volatility and drawdown. That helped some during the bond bull market of the past
30 years, but it may not be the prudent thing to do now. Risk parity, which
substitutes other risks for reduced volatility from equities, takes this to an
extreme and may be ill timed now in today's low-interest-rate environment.

Everything-but-the-kitchen-sink diversification may also be disap-
pointing in the years ahead. Too much diversification can lead to medio-
cre returns due to the lack of decent risk premium. As Warren Buffett said,
"Diversification may preserve wealth, but concentration builds wealth."

Those who have been paying close attention to academic research might
realize that value and small-cap investing may no longer offer good opportunities for abnormal profits. The same may be true of smart beta, which often
turns out to be not very smart after all.

Under the old paradigm, investors who stand the best chance of succeeding are those using low-cost, passively managed index funds as recommended by Warren Buffett, Charles Schwab, John Bogle, Bernie Madoff
(okay, forget Bernie Madoff), and others.[1] Yet passive index funds are still

subject to large drawdowns. They also may still trigger emotional responses and create unwise investor behavior at inopportune times.

NEW INVESTMENT PARADIGM

In contrast to this old hit-and-miss paradigm, our new dual momentum paradigm puts us in harmony with market forces. It uses simple ideas that work in the real world and are easy to implement.

Due to myopic loss aversion and too much focus on short-term return variability, investors may hold more bonds than they should in order to maximize their long-run wealth. This aversion to equities has led to a higher equity risk premium.

With dual momentum, we can comfortably focus more on equities, especially U.S. equities, and capture this higher-risk premium. We still use fixed income with its lower expected return, but we use it primarily when equities are weak and it makes the most sense to hold bonds.

Our new paradigm uses relative strength momentum to enhance returns by taking advantage of intramarket trends. More importantly, our new paradigm uses absolute momentum to ensure that those trends are positive and to reduce the large drawdowns that would still exist if one used only relative momentum.

It is this elegant combination of relative and absolute momentum that translates overall into higher expected returns with lower expected risk. Dual momentum helps remove emotional and behavioral biases in others from the decision-making process. In fact, it allows us to take advantage of these biases instead of having them adversely affect us.

CONTINUING EFFECTIVENESS OF MOMENTUM

The outperformance of momentum over the past 200 years of data across dozens of markets and asset classes suggests that the momentum anomaly is not just a short-lived one. Since dual momentum is such a good thing, it might be natural to wonder if it might lose its effectiveness when more people finally discover and start using it. Of course, any anomaly can lose some profitability once it starts to be widely followed. However, the deep-seated behavioral biases behind momentum are quite strong, and human nature does not easily change. Furthermore, due to human inertia and lingering ignorance, it is unlikely that the majority of people will suddenly wake up and become enthusiastic momentum investors. This should help keep many investors trading against momentum rather than with it.

As an indication of this, the performance of actively managed funds in aggregate is clearly inferior to the performance of passively managed funds, due largely to the higher costs of active management.[2] People have known this for many years, yet over 70% of all funds are still actively managed.[3] Similarly, ETFs have many advantages over mutual funds, such as intraday liquidity, lower expense ratios, and preferential tax treatment. Yet there is only $1.62 trillion invested in ETFs compared to $14.8 trillion invested in mutual funds.

Momentum may very well show this same kind of disconnect. Some of those to whom I have explained dual momentum do not appreciate it as the "premier anomaly," and regard it as a niche rather than as a core investment strategy. There are several possible reasons for this. First, I may be a terrible communicator. (For the sake of those buying this book, I hope that is not the case.) Then there are the usual behavioral biases of anchoring and conservatism with respect to something new. Investors are slow to learn and prefer the familiar to the unfamiliar. Next is skepticism by some regarding the efficacy of trend-following methods like absolute momentum. Furthermore, one usually has to invest some time and energy to really understand and appreciate the benefits of dual momentum investing. I hope that this book will help in that regard. Those willing to take the time and make the required effort should have a substantial advantage over most other investors.

CHALLENGES AND OPPORTUNITIES

There will undoubtedly be periods when dual momentum underperforms its benchmarks. During those times, investors may lose sight of the big picture and be tempted to behave in ways that hurt them in the long run.

The main challenge facing dual momentum investors in the future may very well be their own willingness to follow the model patiently and with the requisite discipline. It is human nature to want to tinker and attempt to add value even when it is impossible to do so. Unfortunately, because of over-confidence, we tend to overweight our own opinions so that most "enhance-ment" efforts actually end up being counterproductive.

Grove et al. (2000) did a meta-analysis, or study of studies, on 136 published papers across a wide range of professions in which they ana-lyzed the accuracy of quantitative models versus expert judgment.[4] Models beat experts 94% of the time. Human judgment prevailed over quantita-tive models in only eight studies, and all of these had access to informa-tion not available to the quantitative models. Even when given access to the quantitative model results, experts still underperformed the models. Quantitative models had become a floor rather than a ceiling. According to Grove et al., "Humans are susceptible to many errors in clinical judg-ment. These include ignoring base rates, assigning nonoptimal weights to cues, failure to take into account regression toward the mean, and failure to properly assess covariation."[5]

Jim Simons, the billionaire founder of Renaissance Technologies and Medallion Fund, is one of the best systems traders on the planet. His per-sonal income in 2013 from managing his hedge funds was $2.2 billion. Simons says, "So if you're going to trade using models, you should just slav-ishly use the models. You do whatever the hell it says no matter how smart or dumb you think it is now."[6]

I have learned through my experiences with dual momentum the importance of firmly adhering to a proven, disciplined approach that has clearly shown it can successfully adapt to different market conditions. I have also come to recognize that I am no match for dual momentum and to value it as my best investment friend.

In the words of Richard Driehaus, "The stock market is like a woman. You observe her. You respond to her. And you respect her."[7] That is not as easy as it sounds. Just ask my ex-wife.

Dual momentum gives one the framework for accomplishing this. It has helped me to respond appropriately and confidently to market forces, and it can help you do the same. In the words of Victor Hugo, "The future has many names. For the weak, it means the unattainable. For the fearful, it means the unknown. For the courageous, it means opportunity." I wish you all the best on your own dual momentum–based journey.

ALL ABOARD!

Momentum is like being on an express train bound for the riches of Golconda. On this journey, our main rolling stock is the *Equities Special*. If it is passed by a faster-moving train, we hop on over to keep moving forward as quickly as possible. Occasionally, all equity trains come to a stop and go into reverse. When that happens, we're going to ride with old Railroad "Treasury" Bill, who moves along slow and steady. Once the *Equities Special* gets moving along nicely again, we return to it, settle back down, and enjoy the rewarding ride.

On our pleasant journey, we swiftly pass the *Lake Wobegon Flyer*, actively engineered by former mutual fund managers who all think they are better than each other. We speed by the *Buy and Behold Line*, with its efficient conductor who randomly walks around shouting, "Damn the torpedoes, full speed ahead!" That would be appropriate if he were conducting a smooth-sailing ship, but he has to instead traverse the ups and downs of many hills and valleys, which can cause passenger distress.

We pass a trainyard full of expensive, hedged wrecks and long/short conveyances going around and around in silly circles, getting nowhere fast. With not so much to power it now, the *Commodities Caboose* falls far behind after some bumpy rides hither and yon. We pass the *Managed Futures Limited* that just ran out of steam, and there lies the steel-drivin' man, John Henry, along with Casey "Tudor" Jones.

Finally, we come to *Dante's Station* with its flashing sign, "Abandon All Hope, You Who Enter Here." "Dazed and Confused" blares from the loudspeakers. We sing out to the poor souls who are sitting on their assets doing nothing now:

> Now listen to the jingle, and the rumble, and the roar,
> as she dashes thro' the woodland, and speeds along the shore,
> See the mighty rushing engine, hear the merry bell ring out,
> as we speed along in safety, on the Dual Momentum Route.[8]

GLOBAL EQUITY MOMENTUM

MONTHLY RESULTS

Table A.1   Global Equities Momentum

	JAN.	FEB.	MAR.	APR.	MAY	JUNE	JULY	AUG.	SEPT.	OCT.	NOV.	DEC.	GEM ANNUAL	ACWI ANNUAL
1974	0.4	0.3	-2.5	-1.9	0.8	-2.3	-0.4	-1.4	1.9	4.3	1.0	0.2	0.2	-24.5
1975	4.0	1.7	-1.9	-1.1	2.3	4.8	-6.4	-1.8	-3.1	6.5	2.5	-0.8	6.1	34.5
1976	12.2	-0.8	3.4	-0.8	-1.1	4.4	-0.5	-0.2	2.6	-1.9	-0.4	5.6	23.9	14.7
1977	-4.7	-1.8	0.7	0.9	0.7	1.4	-0.1	1.0	0.0	-0.5	0.9	-0.4	-2.1	2.0
1978	-0.2	0.4	0.3	0.1	-0.5	4.1	1.1	2.1	3.0	4.9	1.0	-1.0	16.4	18.2
1979	1.9	-0.1	2.9	-0.1	-1.3	2.2	0.6	-0.3	4.9	-8.2	4.8	2.1	9.0	12.7
1980	6.2	0.0	-9.7	11.3	4.7	3.2	0.1	1.0	3.7	2.0	-1.4	-3.0	17.9	27.7
1981	-4.2	1.7	4.0	-1.9	0.3	-0.6	0.2	-2.1	-0.1	5.9	8.5	-3.7	7.4	-3.3
1982	0.6	2.0	1.3	2.8	1.6	-1.6	4.3	5.5	4.0	5.3	4.0	1.9	36.5	11.3
1983	3.7	2.3	3.7	7.9	-0.9	3.9	-3.0	1.5	1.4	-1.2	3.3	3.7	29.3	23.3
1984	3.3	1.4	7.9	-0.2	-3.1	1.3	4.5	1.7	2.4	4.2	1.8	1.5	29.7	5.8
1985	2.3	1.2	0.1	-0.1	5.8	1.6	-0.1	2.8	4.9	5.8	4.4	4.3	37.9	41.8
1986	2.4	10.4	13.6	6.2	-4.2	6.3	5.6	9.7	-0.9	-6.3	5.6	5.1	65.8	42.8
1987	10.8	3.1	8.5	10.0	-0.1	-2.9	0.4	7.1	-1.5	-14.5	0.8	1.4	22.5	16.8
1988	3.5	1.2	-0.9	-0.5	-0.7	2.4	-0.5	0.3	2.3	1.9	5.6	0.6	15.9	24.0
1989	2.0	0.4	-1.7	5.2	4.0	-0.6	9.0	2.0	-0.4	-2.3	2.0	2.4	23.8	17.7
1990	-6.7	1.3	2.6	-2.5	9.8	-0.7	-0.3	-1.3	0.8	1.3	2.2	1.6	7.4	-16.5
1991	1.2	7.2	2.4	0.2	4.3	-4.6	4.7	2.4	-1.7	1.3	-4.0	11.4	26.6	19.9
1992	-1.9	1.3	-1.9	2.9	0.5	-1.5	4.1	-2.0	1.2	0.3	3.4	1.2	7.6	-4.2
1993	0.8	1.4	2.1	-2.4	2.2	-1.2	3.3	5.4	-2.1	3.6	-7.6	7.8	13.2	24.9
1994	8.2	-0.8	-4.6	-0.8	0.0	0.7	2.0	3.4	-2.5	-0.1	-0.2	0.7	5.7	5.0
1995	2.0	2.4	3.0	2.9	4.0	2.3	3.3	0.3	4.2	-0.4	4.4	1.9	34.8	19.5
1996	3.4	0.9	1.0	1.5	2.6	0.4	-4.4	2.1	5.6	2.8	7.6	-2.0	23.0	13.2
1997	6.2	0.8	-4.1	6.0	6.1	4.5	8.0	-5.6	5.5	-3.3	4.6	1.7	33.4	15.0

	JAN.	FEB.	MAR.	APR.	MAY	JUNE	JULY	AUG.	SEPT.	OCT.	NOV.	DEC.	GEM ANNUAL	ACWI ANNUAL
1998	1.1	7.2	5.1	1.0	-1.7	4.1	-1.1	-14.5	6.4	8.1	6.1	5.8	28.6	22.0
1999	4.2	-3.1	4.0	3.9	-2.4	5.5	-3.1	-0.5	-2.7	3.7	2.0	9.5	22.1	26.8
2000	-5.4	2.7	3.8	-5.6	-2.6	4.3	-3.9	1.2	-5.3	-0.4	1.6	1.9	-8.2	-14.0
2001	1.6	0.9	0.5	-0.4	0.6	0.4	2.2	1.1	1.2	2.1	-1.4	-0.6	8.4	-15.9
2002	0.8	1.0	-1.7	1.9	0.8	0.9	1.2	1.7	1.6	-0.5	0.0	2.1	10.3	-19.0
2003	0.1	1.4	-0.1	0.8	1.9	-0.2	-3.4	2.0	2.8	6.5	2.2	7.6	23.3	34.6
2004	1.6	2.5	0.6	-3.1	0.3	2.2	-2.9	0.8	3.2	3.5	6.9	4.3	21.4	15.8
2005	-1.7	4.9	-2.7	-2.5	0.6	1.9	3.7	2.6	5.2	-3.6	3.4	4.8	17.1	11.4
2006	7.0	-0.3	2.9	5.2	-4.6	-0.1	1.0	2.8	0.1	4.1	3.6	3.1	27.2	21.5
2007	0.4	0.6	2.8	4.6	2.7	0.9	-0.3	-1.5	6.6	5.6	-4.5	-1.4	17.1	12.2
2008	-9.7	0.1	0.3	-0.2	-0.7	-0.1	-0.1	0.9	-1.3	-2.4	3.3	3.7	-6.5	-41.9
2009	-0.9	-0.4	1.4	0.5	0.7	0.6	1.6	1.0	1.1	0.5	2.9	2.1	11.6	35.4
2010	-4.9	0.0	6.9	-0.8	-10.4	-5.2	7.0	-4.5	8.9	3.8	0.0	6.7	5.5	13.2
2011	2.4	3.4	0.0	3.0	-2.8	-1.4	-2.0	-5.4	-7.0	10.9	-0.2	1.0	0.7	-6.9
2012	4.5	4.3	3.3	-0.6	-6.0	0.0	1.4	2.3	2.6	-1.9	0.6	0.9	11.4	16.8
2013	4.1	1.4	3.8	1.9	2.3	-1.3	5.1	-2.9	3.1	4.6	3.1	2.5	31.0	23.4

Global Equities Momentum (GEM) is a rule-based approach using relative and absolute momentum applied to the following indices: Standard & Poor's 500, MSCI All Country World ex-US (MSCI World ex-US prior to 1988) and Barclays Capital U.S. Aggregate Bond. GEM is reconstituted monthly. You cannot invest directly in GEM. Performance does not represent actual fund or portfolio performance. All performance represents total returns and includes reinvestment of interest and dividends but does not reflect possible management fees, transaction costs, taxes, or other expenses. Historical data and analysis should not be taken as an indication or guarantee of any future performance.

ABSOLUTE MOMENTUM: A SIMPLE RULE-BASED STRATEGY AND UNIVERSAL TREND-FOLLOWING OVERLAY

ABSTRACT

There is a considerable body of research on relative strength price momentum but much less on absolute momentum, also known as time-series momentum. In this paper, we explore the practical side of absolute momentum. We first explore its sole parameter—the formation, or look-back, period. We then examine the reward, risk, and correlation characteristics of absolute momentum applied to stocks, bonds, and real assets. We finally apply absolute momentum to a 60/40 stock/bond portfolio and a simple risk parity portfolio. We show that absolute momentum can effectively identify regime change and add significant value as an easy-to-implement, rule-based approach with many potential uses as both a stand-alone program and trend-following overlay.

INTRODUCTION

The momentum effect is one of the strongest and most pervasive financial phenomena (Jegadeesh and Titman 1993, 2001). Researchers have verified its value with many different asset classes, as well as across groups of assets (Blitz and Van Vliet 2008; Asness, Moskowitz and Pedersen (2013). Since its publication, relative strength momentum has held up out-of-sample going forward in time (Grundy and Martin 2001; Asness et al. 2013) and back to the year 1801 (Geczy and Samonov 2012).

In addition to relative strength momentum, in which an asset's performance relative to its peers predicts its future relative performance, momentum also works well on an absolute or time-series basis in which an asset's own past return predicts its future performance. In absolute momentum, we look only at an asset's excess return over a given look-back period. In absolute momentum, there is significant positive auto-covariance between an asset's return in the following month and its past one-year excess return (Moskowitz, Ooi and Pedersen 2012).

Absolute momentum is therefore trend following by nature. Trend-following methods, in general, have slowly achieved recognition and acceptance in the academic community (Brock, Lakonishok and LeBaron 1992; Lo, Mamaysky, and Wang 2000; Zhu and Zhou 2009; Han, Yang, and Zhou 2011).

Absolute momentum appears to be just as robust and universally applicable as relative momentum. It performs well in extreme market environments, across multiple asset classes (commodities, equity indexes, bond markets, currency pairs), and back in time to the turn of the century (Hurst, Ooi, and Pedersen 2012).

Despite an abundance of momentum research over the past 20 years, no one is sure why it works. Brown and Jennings (1989) developed a rational equilibrium-based model using historical prices with technical analysis. More recently, Zhou and Zhu (2014) identified equilibrium returns due to the risk-sharing function provided by trend-following trading rules, such as absolute momentum.

The most common explanations for both momentum and trend-following profits, however, have to do with behavioral factors, such as anchoring, herding, and the disposition effect (Tversky and Kahneman 1974; Barberis, Shleifer, and Vishny 1998; Daniel, Hirshleifer, and Subrahmanyam 1998; Hong and Stein 1999; Frazzini 2006).

In anchoring, investors are slow to react to new information, which leads initially to underreaction. In herding, buying begets more buying and causes prices to overreact and move beyond fundamental value after the initial underreaction. Through the disposition effect, investors sell winners too soon and hold losers too long. This creates a headwind, making trends continue longer before reaching true value.

Risk management schemes that sell in down markets and buy in up markets can also cause trends to persist (Gârleanu and Pedersen 2007), as can confirmation bias, which causes investors to look at recent price moves as representative of the future. This then leads them to move money into investments that have recently appreciated, thus causing trends to continue further (Tversky and Kahneman 1974). Behavioral biases are deeply rooted, which may explain why momentum profits have persisted and may continue to persist.

In this paper, we focus on absolute momentum because of its simplicity and the advantages it holds for long-only investing. We can apply absolute momentum to any asset or portfolio of assets without losing any of the contributory value of other assets. With relative strength momentum, on the other hand, we exclude or reduce the influence of some assets from the active portfolio. This can diminish the benefits that come from multiasset diversification and lead to opportunity loss by excluding lagging assets that may suddenly start outperforming.

The second advantage of absolute momentum is its superior ability to reduce downside volatility by identifying regime change. Both relative and absolute momentum can enhance return, but absolute momentum, unlike relative momentum, is also effective in reducing the downside exposure associated with long-only investing (Antonacci 2012).

The next section of this paper describes our data and the methodology we use to work with absolute momentum. The following section explores the formation period used for determining absolute momentum. After that, we show what effect absolute momentum has on the reward, risk, and correlation characteristics of a number of diverse markets, compared to a buy and hold approach. Finally, we apply absolute momentum to two representative multiasset portfolios—a 60/40 balanced stock/bond portfolio and a simple, diversified risk parity portfolio.

DATA AND METHODOLOGY

All monthly data begins in January 1973, unless otherwise noted, and includes interest and dividends. For equities, we use the MSCI (Morgan Stanley Capital International) US and MSCI EAFE (Europe, Australia, and Far East) indexes. These are free-float-adjusted market capitalization weightings of large and mid-cap stocks. For fixed income, we use the Barclays Capital Long U.S. Treasury, Intermediate U.S. Treasury, U.S. Credit, U.S. High Yield Corporate, U.S. Government & Credit, and U.S. Aggregate Bond indexes. The beginning date of the high-yield index is July 1, 1983, and the start date of the aggregate bond index is January 1, 1976. For dates prior to January 1976, we substitute the Government & Credit index for the Aggregate Bond index, since they track one another closely. For Treasury bills, we use the monthly returns on 90-day U.S. Treasury bill holdings. For real assets, we use the FTSE NAREIT U.S. Real Estate index, the Standard & Poor's GSCI (formally Goldman Sachs Commodity Index), and monthly gold returns based on the month-end closing London PM gold fix.

Although there are more complicated methods for determining absolute momentum (Baltas and Kosowski 2012), our strategy simply defines absolute momentum as being positive when the excess return (asset return less the Treasury bill return) over the formation (look-back) period is positive. We hold a long position in our selected assets during these times. When absolute momentum turns negative (i.e., an asset's excess return turns negative), our baseline strategy is to exit the asset and switch into 90-day U.S. Treasury bills until absolute momentum again becomes positive. Treasury bills are a safe harbor for us during times of market stress.

We reevaluate and adjust positions monthly. The number of transactions per year into or out of Treasury bills ranges from a low of 0.33 for REITs to a high of 1.08 for high-yield bonds. We deduct 20 basis points for transaction costs for each switch into or out of Treasury bills.[1] Maximum drawdown is the greatest peak-to-valley equity erosion on a month-end basis.

FORMATION PERIOD

Table B.1 shows the Sharpe ratios for formation periods ranging from 2 to 18 months. Since our data begins in January 1973 (except for high-yield bonds, which begin in July 1983) and 18 months is the maximum formation period that we consider, results extend from July 1974 through December 2012. We have highlighted the highest Sharpe ratios for each asset. Best results cluster at 12 months. As a check on this, we segment our data into subsamples and find the highest Sharpe ratios for each asset in every decade from 1974 through 2012. Figure B.1 shows the number of times the Sharpe ratio is highest, or within two percentage points of being highest, for each look-back period across all the decades.

Both our aggregated and segmented results coincide with the best formation periods of relative momentum, which extend from 3 to 12 months and cluster at 12 months (Jegadeesh and Titman 1993).[2] Many momentum research papers use a 12-month formation period with a one-month holding period as a benchmark strategy for research purposes. Given its dominance here and throughout the literature, we also use a 12-month formation period as our benchmark strategy. This should minimize transaction costs and the risk of data snooping.

Table B.1   Formation Period Sharpe Ratios

Look-Back	18	16	14	12	10	8	6	4	2
MSCI US	0.41	0.43	0.45	0.56	0.46	0.44	0.41	0.38	0.23
EAFE	0.33	0.32	0.35	0.41	0.45	0.32	0.38	0.36	0.46
TBOND	0.40	0.42	0.45	0.54	0.38	0.36	0.33	0.42	0.40
CREDIT	0.75	0.80	0.70	0.74	0.80	0.81	0.69	0.71	0.66
HI YLD	0.70	0.87	0.82	0.92	0.66	0.69	0.82	0.77	0.77
REIT	0.65	0.71	0.72	0.69	0.63	0.63	0.87	0.68	0.63
GSCI	0.04	0.04	0.09	0.20	0.09	−0.08	−0.11	0.13	0.06
GOLD	0.39	0.35	0.35	0.42	0.39	0.37	0.32	0.30	0.21

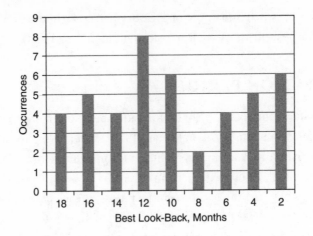

Figure B.1   Best Formation Periods, 1974–2012

ABSOLUTE MOMENTUM CHARACTERISTICS

Table B.2 is a performance summary of each asset and the median of all the assets, with and without 12-month absolute momentum, from January 1974 through December 2012.

Table B.2   Absolute Momentum Results, 1974–2012

	Annual Return	Annual Std Dev	Annual Sharpe	Maximum Drawdown	% Profit, Months
MSCI US Abs Mom	12.26	11.57	0.55	–22.90	75
MSCI US No Mom	11.62	15.74	0.37	–50.65	61
EAFE Abs Mom	10.39	11.82	0.39	–25.14	78
EAFE No Mom	11.56	17.53	0.33	–56.40	60
TBOND Abs Mom	10.08	8.43	0.52	–12.92	77
TBOND No Mom	9.74	10.54	0.39	–20.08	61
CREDIT Abs Mom	8.91	4.72	0.70	–8.70	82
CREDIT No Mom	8.77	7.18	0.44	–19.26	67
HI YLD Abs Mom	9.97	4.76	0.90	–7.14	88
HI YLD No Mom	10.05	8.70	0.50	–33.31	75
REIT Abs Mom	14.16	11.74	0.69	–19.97	75
REIT No Mom	14.74	17.25	0.50	–68.30	62

	Annual Return	Annual Std Dev	Annual Sharpe	Maximum Drawdown	% Profit, Months
GSCI Abs Mom	8.24	15.46	0.17	−48.93	81
GSCI No Mom	4.93	19.96	−0.02	−61.03	54
GOLD Abs Mom	13.68	16.62	0.46	−24.78	81
GOLD No Mom	9.44	19.97	0.19	−61.78	53
MEDIAN Abs Mom	10.25	11.66	0.53	−21.43	79
MEDIAN No Mom	9.90	16.48	0.38	−53.53	61

Figure B.2 shows the Sharpe ratios and percentage of profitable months for these assets, with and without 12-month absolute momentum. Figure B.3 presents the percentage of profitable months, and Figure B.4 shows maximum monthly drawdown. Every asset has a higher Sharpe ratio, lower maximum drawdown, and higher percentage of profitable months with 12-month absolute momentum over this 38-year period.

Table B.3 shows the monthly correlations between our assets, with and without the application of absolute momentum. The average correlation

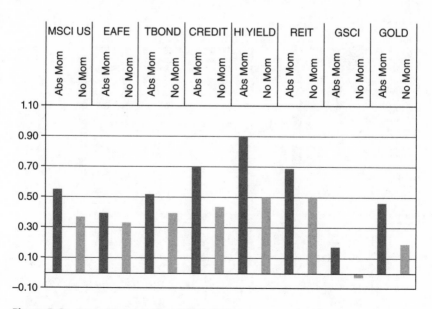

Figure B.2   Asset Sharpe Ratios, 1974–2012

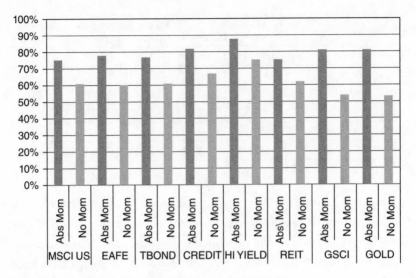

Figure B.3   Percentage of Profitable Months, 1974–2012

of the eight assets without absolute momentum is 0.22, and with absolute momentum, it is 0.21. There is no indication from our data that absolute momentum, in general, increases correlation. This has positive implications for applying absolute momentum to multiasset portfolios, which we look at next.

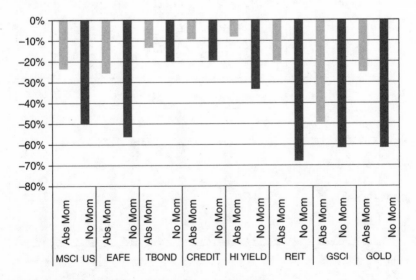

Figure B.4   Maximum Monthly Drawdown, 1974–2012

Table B.3   Monthly Correlations, 1974–2012

No Momentum							
	EAFE	**TBOND**	**CREDIT**	**HI YLD**	**REIT**	**GSCI**	**GOLD**
MSCI US	0.63	0.11	0.26	0.43	0.58	0.10	0.01
EAFE		0.03	0.12	0.37	0.48	0.18	0.19
TBOND			0.67	0.12	0.05	−0.10	0.01
CREDIT				0.40	0.15	0.04	−0.02
HI YLD.					0.32	0.07	−0.04
REIT						0.11	0.07
GSCI							0.27
12-Month Absolute Momentum							
	EAFE	**TBOND**	**CREDIT**	**HI YLD**	**REIT**	**GSCI**	**GOLD**
MSCI US	0.49	0.05	0.35	0.45	0.45	0.14	0.04
EAFE		0.03	0.26	0.31	0.29	0.13	0.11
TBOND			0.81	0.04	−0.03	−0.04	−0.02
CREDIT				0.38	0.28	−0.01	0.05
HI YLD.					0.41	0.09	0.02
REIT						0.13	0.12
GSCI							0.30

Figures B.5 through B.12 are log-scale growth charts of each asset with a starting value of 100.

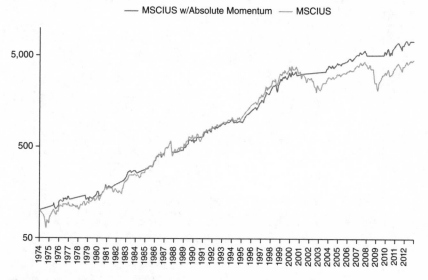

Figure B.5   MSCI US, 1974–2012

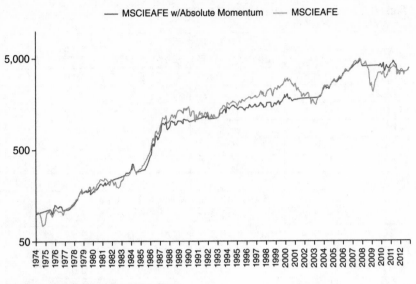

Figure B.6   MSCI EAFE, 1974–2012

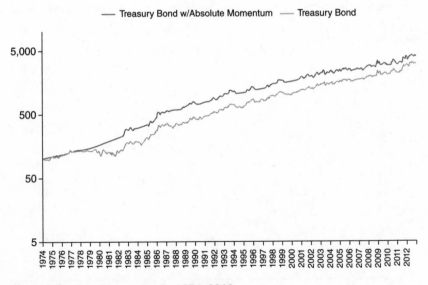

Figure B.7   U.S. Treasury Bonds, 1974–2012

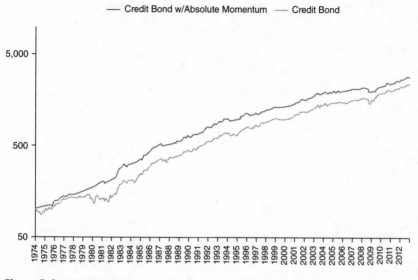

Figure B.8   U.S. Credit Bonds, 1974–2012

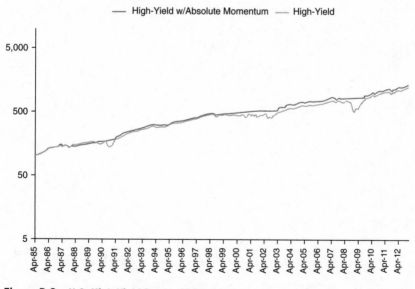

Figure B.9   U.S. High-Yield Bonds, 1984–2012

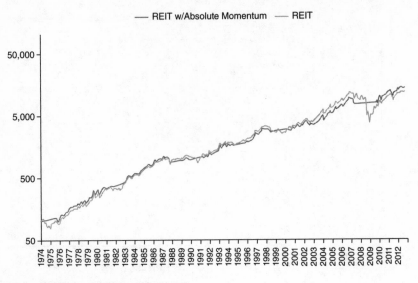

Figure B.10   U.S. REITs, 1974–2012

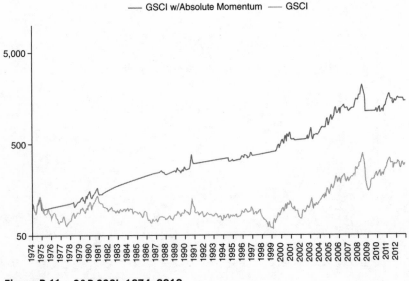

Figure B.11   S&P GSCI, 1974–2012

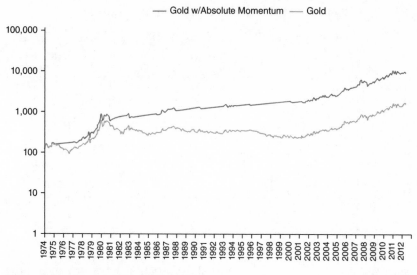

Figure B.12   London Gold, 1974–2012

60/40 BALANCED PORTFOLIO

Given the ability of 12-month absolute momentum to improve risk-adjusted performance over a broad range of individual assets, it is natural to wonder how absolute momentum might affect our multiasset portfolios. One of the simplest multiasset portfolios is the 60% stocks and 40% bonds mix (60/40) that institutional investors adopted in the mid-1960s, based on their observation of stock and bond returns from 1926 through 1965. Table B.4 shows how a 60/40 portfolio of the MSCI US and U.S. Treasury indexes, as well as the MSCI US index, have performed since 1974, with and without the addition of 12-month absolute momentum.

The 60/40 portfolio without momentum shows some reduction in volatility and drawdown compared to an investment solely in U.S. stocks. However, the strong 0.92 monthly correlation of the 60/40 portfolio with the S&P 500 shows that the 60/40 portfolio has retained most of the market risk of stocks. Because stocks are much more volatile than bonds, stock market movement dominates the risk in a 60/40 portfolio. From a risk perspective, the regular 60/40 portfolio is, in fact, mostly an equity portfolio, since

Table B.4   60/40 Balanced Portfolio Performance, 1974–2012

	Annual Return	Annual Std Dev	Annual Sharpe	Max. Drawdown	% Profit Months	Correlation to S&P 500	Correlation to 10-Yr. Bond
60/40 w/abs mom	11.52	7.88	0.72	−13.45	74	0.67	0.37
60/40 No mom	10.86	10.77	0.47	−29.32	63	0.92	0.46
MSCI US w/abs mom	12.26	11.57	0.55	−22.90	75	0.74	0.13
MSCI US no mom	11.62	15.74	0.37	−50.65	61	1.00	0.10

stock market variation explains most of the variation in performance of the 60/40 portfolio.

The MSCI US index with the addition of absolute momentum has a 0.74 correlation to the S&P 500, which is lower than the 0.92 correlation of the 60/40 index to the S&P 500. MSCI US with absolute momentum does a better job than the 60/40 portfolio in reducing portfolio drawdown, while also providing higher returns. The correlation to the S&P 500 of the 60/40 portfolio using 12-month absolute momentum drops to 0.67 from 0.92.[3] The 60/40 portfolio with absolute momentum retains the same return as the normal MSCI US Index, but with only half the volatility. The maximum drawdown drops by more than 70%.

Figure B.13 shows the maximum 1, 3, 6, and 12-month drawdown of the MSCI US index and the 60/40 portfolios, with and without 12-month absolute momentum. Figure B.14 is a rolling five-year window of the maximum drawdown of the same portfolios.

The traditional 60/40 portfolio offers little in the way of risk-reducing diversification, even though it looks balanced from the perspective of dollars invested in each asset class. From 1900 through 2012, the probability of the 60/40 portfolio having a negative real return has been 35% in any one year, 20% over any five years, and 10% over any 10 years.[4] Its real maximum drawdown was 66%. Adding a simple 12-month absolute momentum overlay to the 60/40 portfolio achieves market-level returns with a

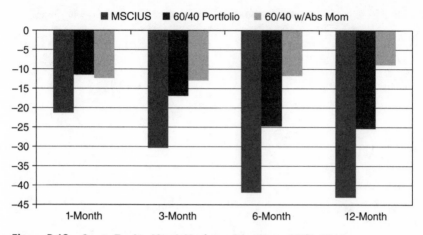

Figure B.13   One to Twelve-Month Maximum Drawdown, 1974–2012

more reasonable amount of downside risk. Figure B.15 shows the consistency of the 12-month absolute momentum 60/40 portfolio compared to the traditional 60/40 portfolio. The trend-following, market-timing feature of absolute momentum may be more valuable now than in the past, when the world was less interconnected, asset correlations were lower, and diversification alone was better able to reduce downside exposure.

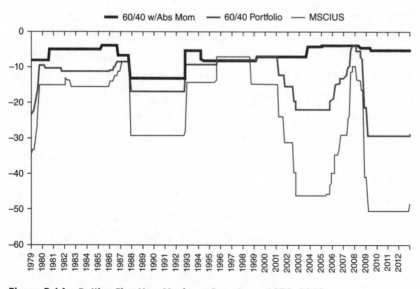

Figure B.14   Rolling Five-Year Maximum Drawdown, 1979–2012

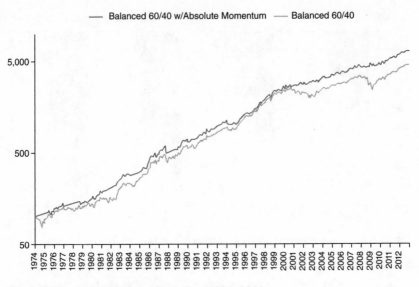

Figure B.15   60/40 Balanced Portfolios, 1974–2012

PARITY PORTFOLIOS

The usual way of dealing with the strong equities tilt of the 60/40 portfolio is to diversify more broadly and/or dedicate a larger allocation to fixed-income investments. Endowment funds, for example, often diversify into a number of specialized areas, such as private equity, hedge funds, and other higher-risk alternative investments. Some risk parity programs also diversify broadly. In addition, risk parity portfolios attempt to equalize the risk across different asset classes by allocating more capital to relatively lower-volatility assets, like fixed income. A stock/bond portfolio, for example, would require at least a 70% allocation to bonds in order to have equal risk exposure from bonds and equities.

A common way to construct risk parity portfolios is to weight each asset's position size by the inverse of its volatility.[5] This normalizes risk exposure across all asset classes. But there are several problems with that approach. First, one somehow has to determine the best look-back interval and frequency for measuring volatility. This introduces data-snooping bias.

Second, volatility and correlation are inherently unstable and nonstationary. Their use therefore introduces additional estimation risk and potential portfolio instability. We take a simpler approach that accomplishes much the same thing as traditional risk parity. Starting with the MSCI US and long Treasury bond indexes used in our 60/40 portfolio, we add REITs, credit bonds, and gold, with an equal weighting given to each asset class.[6] We use credit bonds to increase the fixed-income exposure of the portfolio. Credit bonds diversify our fixed-income allocation by providing some credit risk premium with less duration risk than long Treasuries. REITs give us exposure to real assets with some additional risk exposure to equities. Gold gives us real asset exposure that is different from real estate.[7] Gold has the highest volatility, and so it represents only 20% of our parity portfolio, whereas bonds receive the largest allocation of 40%, being represented twice in the portfolio. Exposure to equities is somewhere between gold and bonds.

By structuring our portfolio purposefully to begin with, we are able to balance our risk exposure between fixed income, equities, and real assets nonparametrically without incurring any added estimation risk. We will see that the addition of absolute momentum to our parity portfolio reduces and equalizes risk exposure across all asset classes.

Table B.5 shows the correlations of the S&P 500, U.S. 10 Year Treasury, and GSCI Commodity indexes to the 60/40 and parity portfolios, both with and without 12-month absolute momentum. Our parity portfolio with 12-month absolute momentum shows a modest and nearly equal correlation to both stocks and bonds. Because of the downside risk attenuation through absolute momentum, we have achieved risk parity while limiting fixed-income assets to no more than 40% of our portfolio.

Table B.5 Monthly Correlations, 1974–2012

	60/40 Portfolio	60/40 w/Abs Momentum	Parity Portfolio	Parity w/Abs Momentum
S&P 500	0.92	0.67	0.67	0.40
10-yr Treasury	0.58	0.35	0.37	0.36
GSCI	0.05	0.06	0.25	0.19

Having a well-balanced portfolio means that in low-growth and low-inflation environments, bonds may outperform and sustain the portfolio, whereas equities and REITs may perform better and sustain the portfolio under high-inflation and high-growth scenarios. Table B.6 shows the comparative performance of the 60/40 and parity portfolios, with and without 12-month absolute momentum, overall and by decade. The parity portfolio with absolute momentum maintains the highest Sharpe ratio and the lowest drawdown throughout the data. Figure B.16 is a chart of the parity portfolio versus the 60/40 balanced portfolio, and Figure B.17 shows the parity portfolio versus its components.

Table B.6   Parity Portfolios Versus 60/40 Balanced Portfolios, 1974–2012

	Parity w/Abs Mom	Parity Portfolio	60/40 w/Abs Mom	60/40 Portfolio
All Data				
Annual return	11.98	11.28	11.52	10.86
Annual std dev	5.75	8.88	7.88	10.77
Annual Sharpe	1.06	0.62	0.72	0.47
Max drawdown	−9.60	−30.40	−13.45	−29.32
% Profit, months	75	69	74	63
1974–1983				
Annual return	15.78	13.10	11.37	9.41
Annual std dev	7.20	10.05	6.88	12.35
Annual Sharpe	0.86	0.38	0.33	0.04
Max drawdown	−6.31	−16.89	−8.19	−22.95
% Profit, months	80	64	81	52
1984–1993				
Annual return	12.34	10.19	14.48	15.63
Annual std dev	4.98	5.62	9.78	11.40
Annual Sharpe	1.09	0.62	0.75	0.73
Max drawdown	−4.28	−6.53	−13.45	−16.99
% Profit, months	78	71	79	68

	Parity w/Abs Mom	Parity Portfolio	60/40 w/Abs Mom	60/40 Portfolio
1994–2003				
Annual return	9.06	9.45	12.10	10.86
Annual std dev	4.65	6.66	8.23	10.05
Annual Sharpe	0.99	0.74	0.90	0.62
Max drawdown	−4.87	−7.56	−8.16	−22.14
% Profit, months	72	73	69	64
2004–2012				
Annual return	10.69	12.55	7.84	7.34
Annual std dev	5.78	12.12	5.92	8.80
Annual Sharpe	1.47	0.84	0.99	0.61
Max drawdown	−9.60	−30.40	−5.03	−29.32
% Profit, months	69	70	67	69

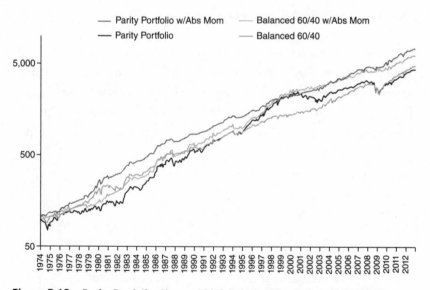

Figure B.16   Parity Portfolios Versus 60/40 Balanced Portfolios, 1974–2012

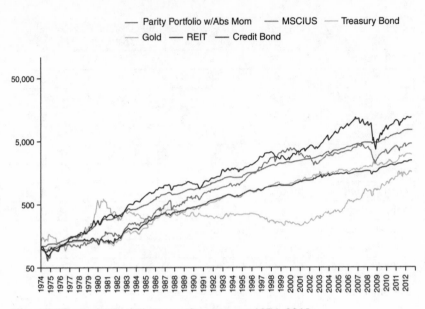

Figure B.17   Parity Portfolio Versus Components, 1974–2012

Figure B.18 is a box plot showing quartile ranges of rolling 12-month portfolio returns. Figure B.19 shows the difference in monthly returns between the parity portfolios with and without 12-month absolute momentum. There was some increased volatility in 2008–2009. However, the plotted trend line shows the average return differences remained constant over time.

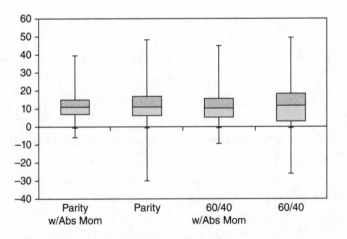

Figure B.18   Rolling 12-Month Returns, 1975–2012

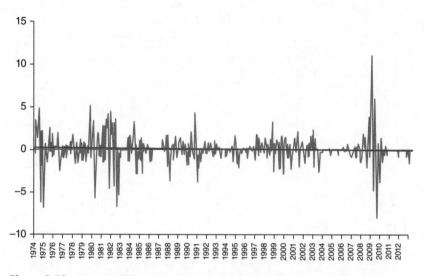

Figure B.19   Monthly Differences in Parity Portfolio Performance, 1974–2012

PARITY PORTFOLIO DRAWDOWN

As was the case with individual assets and the 60/40 portfolio, 12-month absolute momentum excels in reducing the parity portfolio drawdown, as Figures B.20 and B.21 show.

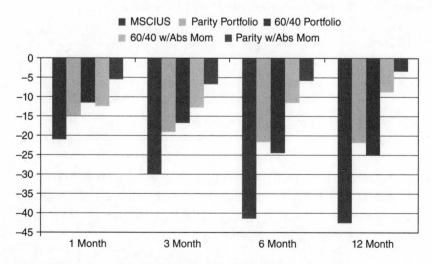

Figure B.20   One- to Twelve-Month Maximum Drawdown, 1974–2012

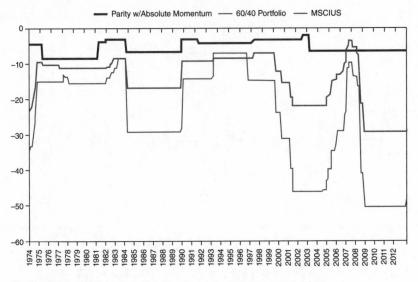

Figure B.21   Rolling Five-Year Maximum Drawdown, 1974–2012

Table B.7 shows how our parity portfolio with absolute momentum, by adapting to regime change, bypassed the major equity erosions of the stock market since our data began in 1974.

Table B.7   Maximum Stock Market Drawdown, 1974–2012

	MSCI US	60/40 Portfolio	Parity w/Abs Mom
3/74–9/74	−33.3	−22.4	+2.2
9/87–11/87	−29.4	−17.0	−1.7
9/00–9/01	−30.9	−15.4	+5.4
4/02–9/02	−29.1	−12.2	+7.3
11/07–2/09	−50.6	−29.3	−0.4

Figure B.22 is a plot of our parity portfolio quarterly returns on the y axis plotted against the corresponding quarterly returns of the S&P 500 index plotted on the x axis. We can see clearly how the parity portfolio with absolute momentum has truncated stock market losses.

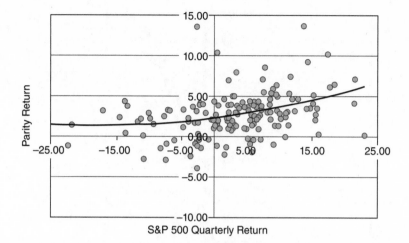

Figure B.22   Quarterly Returns: Parity Portfolio Versus S&P 500, 1974–2012

STOCHASTIC DOMINANCE

Because financial markets can have nonstationary variance and autocorrelated interdependent return distributions, it is best to analyze and compare them using robust or nonparametric methods. One such method is second-order stochastic dominance, where one set of outcomes is preferred over another if it is more predictable (less risky) and has at least as high a mean return (Hader and Russell 1969). Figure B.23 is a plot of the cumulative distribution function of the monthly returns of the parity portfolios, with and without absolute momentum.

The parity portfolio with 12-month absolute momentum shows a lower probability of loss and a greater probability of gain than the parity portfolio without momentum. Because the mean of the parity portfolio with 12-month absolute momentum is also higher than the mean of the parity portfolio without absolute momentum, a risk-averse investor would always prefer the parity portfolio with 12-month absolute momentum, due to second-order stochastic dominance.

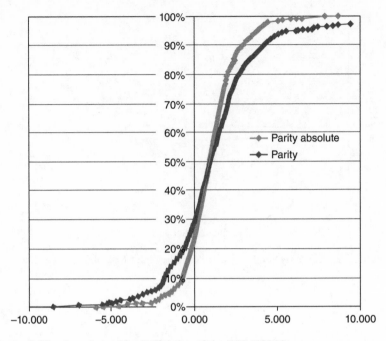

Figure B.23   Cumulative Distribution Functions, 1974–2012

LEVERAGE

Risk parity programs often have so much fixed income in their portfolios that their managers have to leverage the portfolios in order to strive for an acceptable level of expected return. Since absolute momentum reduces the volatility of our parity portfolio while, at the same, preserving equity-level returns, there is not the same need for leverage.

However, given the low expected drawdown of an absolute momentum parity portfolio, one may still wish to use leverage in order to boost expected returns, as is done with other risk parity programs.[8] Table B.8 and Figure B.24 show the pro forma results of our 12-month absolute momentum parity portfolio leveraged to an annual volatility level just below the long-term volatility of a normal 60/40 portfolio. We use a borrowing cost of the fed funds rate plus 25 basis points[9] and a leverage ratio of 1.85 to 1.

Table B.8   Parity Portfolios, 1974–2012

	Leveraged Parity w/Abs Mom	Parity Portfolio w/Abs Mom	Parity Portfolio, No Momentum
Annual return	16.87	11.98	11.28
Annual std dev	10.61	5.75	8.88
Annual Sharpe	0.98	1.06	0.62
Max drawdown	−18.44	−9.60	−30.40
Skewness	0.07	0.16	−0.82
Excess kurtosis	2.77	2.70	7.04

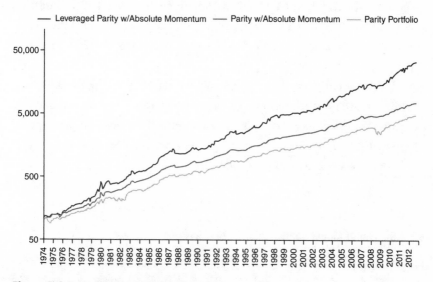

Figure B.24   Parity Portfolios, 1974–2012

Risk in a levered portfolio has many facets, such as fat tail, illiquidity, counterparty, basis, and converging correlation risk. Since most risk parity programs have well over 50% of their assets in fixed-income securities, their greatest future risk may be that of rising interest rates. An increase in nominal interest rates back to a historically normal level of 6% could lead to a 50% drop in the price of long bonds. Parity with 12-month absolute momentum, as presented here, is more adaptive than normal risk parity and has the ability to exit fixed-income investments during periods of rising interest rates due to its trend-following nature. Absolute momentum is, in general, a valuable adjunct to the use of leverage.

FACTOR PRICING MODELS

Table B.9 shows our 12-month absolute momentum parity portfolio regressed against the U.S. stock market using the single-factor capital asset pricing model (CAPM), as well as the three-factor Fama/French model incorporating market, size, and value risk factors, as per the Kenneth French website.[10] We also show a four-factor Fama/French model that adds relative momentum, as well as a six-factor model that additionally adds the excess return of the Barclays Capital U.S. Aggregate Bond and S&P GSCI commodity indexes.

Since our parity portfolio is long only, we naturally see highly significant loadings on the stock, bond, and GSCI market factors. Absolute momentum captures some significant cross-sectional momentum beta. Our parity portfolio with 12-month absolute momentum provides substantial and significant alphas according to all four models.

Table B.9   Factor Model Coefficients, 1974–2012

	Annual Alpha	Market Beta	Small Beta	Value Beta	Momentum Beta	Bond Beta	GSCI Beta	R^2
6-factor model	3.82** (4.10)	0.159** (6.90)	−0.044 (1.51)	0.039 (1.41)	0.078** (2.75)	0.259** (3.28)	0.045** (4.56)	0.23
4-factor Fama/ French	4.07** (4.28)	0.167** (7.84)	−0.061* (2.00)	0.054* (2.01)	0.092** (3.39)	-	-	0.21
3-factor Fama/ French	5.24** (5.99)	0.149** (6.54)	−0.071* (2.38)	−0.017 (0.86)	-	-	-	0.17
1-factor model	4.97** (5.62)	0.139** (6.29)	-	-	-	-	-	0.15

Newey-West (1987) robust t-statistics in parentheses adjust for serial correlation and possible heteroskedasticity. Statistical significance at the 1% and 5% level is denoted by ** and *, respectively.

CONCLUSIONS

Cowles and Jones first presented 12-month momentum to the public in 1937. It has held up remarkably well ever since. Relative strength momentum, looking at performance against one's peers, has attracted the most attention from researchers and investors. Yet relative strength is a secondary way of looking at price strength. Absolute momentum, measuring an asset's performance with respect to its own past, is a more direct way of looking at and utilizing market trends to determine price continuation.

Trend determination through absolute momentum can help one navigate downside risk, take advantage of regime persistence, and achieve higher risk-adjusted returns. Absolute momentum, as used here, is a simple rule-based approach that is easy to implement. One needs only to see if returns relative to Treasury bills have been up or down for the preceding year.

We have seen on 39 years of past data how 12-month absolute momentum can help improve the reward-to-risk characteristics of a broad range of investments. Absolute momentum has considerable value as a tactical overlay to multiasset portfolios, where it has many potential uses. A risk parity portfolio using absolute momentum, due to its modest correlation to traditional investments, such as stocks and bonds, could function either as a core holding or as an alternative asset holding.

Absolute momentum can enhance the expected return and reduce the expected drawdown of core portfolios, as we have shown in this paper. It can help investors with basic stock/bond allocations, such as a 60/40 balanced mix, meet their investment objectives without resorting to excessively large allocations to fixed income that could subject them to substantial interest rate risk. We have seen, in fact, that applying absolute momentum to a stock-only portfolio may reduce or eliminate the need for fixed income as a portfolio diversifier. Investors using absolute momentum can also reduce or eliminate leverage, the selection of riskier assets like hedge funds and private placements, and data-snooping based portfolio constructs that rely on nonstationary and estimation risk–prone correlations and covariances.

There are other potential uses as well for absolute momentum. Simple absolute momentum can be a more cost-effective alternative to managed futures (Hurst, Ooi, and Pedersen 2014). It can also be an attractive alternative to option overwriting by retaining more of the potential for upside appreciation while at the same time providing greater downside protection. Absolute momentum can likewise be an attractive alternative to costly tail-risk hedging. It can reduce the need for aggressive diversification with marginal assets having lower expected returns. If one wishes to achieve higher returns by using riskier assets or by leveraging a portfolio, then 12-month absolute momentum can make that more viable by truncating expected drawdown.

Despite its many possible uses, absolute momentum has yet to attract the attention it deserves as an investment strategy and risk management tool. We have developed variations of and enhancements to 12-month absolute momentum that go beyond the scope of this introductory paper. Yet all investors would do well to become familiar with absolute momentum, since, even in its simplest form as presented here, absolute momentum can be an attractive stand-alone strategy or a powerful tactical overlay for improving the risk-adjusted performance of any asset or portfolio.

NOTES

PREFACE

1. "Why Buy and Hold Doesn't Work Anymore," *Money Magazine*, March 2012.
2. Fama and French (2008).

CHAPTER 1

1. For more than you could ever want to know about the first index mutual fund, see John Bogle's write-up at http://www.vanguard.com/bogle_site/lib/sp19970401.html.
2. Unsustainable growth rates assumptions, such as those occurring in bubbles, challenge rational expectations that underlie the efficient market hypothesis.
3. In Bachelier's work, we find the Chapman-Kolmogorov-Smoluchowski equation for continuous stochastic processes, derivation of the Einstein-Wiener Brownian motion process, and recognition that this process is a solution for the partial differential equation for heat diffusion. Bachelier also developed the rudiments of Markov properties, Fokker-Planck equations, Ito calculus, and Doob's martingales.
4. Lo later coauthored a book called *A Non-Random Walk Down Wall Street* as a rejoinder to Burton Malkiel's popular efficient market tome, *A Random Walk Down Wall Street*.
5. See http://www.berkshirehathaway.com/letters/1988.html.

6. The Federal Reserve Bank of New York organized a $3.62 billion bailout of LTCM in order to avoid a collapse of Wall Street. In his book *When Genius Failed*, Lowenstein (2000) tells the interesting story of the dramatic rise and fall of LTCM, which had two Nobel laureates on its board.

7. See C. Munger, "A Lesson on Elementary Worldly Wisdom as It Relates to Investment Management and Business," Lecture at the University of Southern California, Marshall School of Business, 1994.

8. See D. Sutton, "The Berkshire Bunch," *Fortune*, October 1998.

9. Speech at the Boston Security Analysts Society, November 15, 2005.

10. See Fama and French (2008).

CHAPTER 2

1. See O'Neil (2009), p. 174.

2. See Covel (2007), *The Complete Turtle Trader: How 23 Novice Investors Became Overnight Millionaires.*

3. See Schwager (2012), pp. 151–152.

4. See "The Whipsaw Song," https://www.youtube.com/watch?v=O0yZG6eoahU.

5. See Fama and French (1988), Lo and MacKinlay (1988), and Jegadeesh (1990).

6. For U.S. equities, see Fama and French (2008); for developed markets, Rouwenhorst (1998), Chan, Hameed, and Tong (2000), and Griffen, Ji, and Martin (2005); for emerging markets, Rouwenhorst (1999); for industries, Moskowitz and Grinblatt (1999) and Asness, Porter, and Stevens (2000); for equity indexes, Asness, Liew, and Stevens (1997); for global government bonds, Asness, Moskowitz, and Pedersen (2013); for corporate bonds, Jostova et al. (2013); for commodities, Pirrong (2005) and Miffre and Rallis (2007); for currencies, Menkoff et al. (2011) and Okunev and White (2000); for real estate, Beracha and Skiba (2011).

7. See Antonacci (2012), Asness et al. (2013), and King, Silver, and Guo (2002).

8. See Fama and French (2008).

9. See http://papers.ssrn.com/sol3/DisplayAbstractSearch.cfm.

CHAPTER 3

1. For more in-depth information on the methods of modern finance, see Ilmanen (2011) and Meucci (2009).

2. These assumptions are that portfolio returns are normally distributed or that investors have a quadratic utility function. Quadratic utility implies unrealistic increasing absolute risk aversion, meaning you become more risk averse as your wealth increases. The popular Sharpe ratio relies on these same assumptions.

3. See Ang (2012) and Jacobs, Müller, and Weber (2014).

4. When someone asked Markowitz how he invests his own money, Markowitz said he keeps half in a stock index fund and half in bonds.

5. They were Jack Treynor, William Sharpe, John Lintner, Jon Mossin, and later, Fischer Black.

6. There are now robust methods to correct for autocorrelation and heteroscedasticity. See Newey and West (1987).

7. The lead author, Campbell Harvey, was a former editor of the prestigious *Journal of Finance*. The title of this working paper, ". . . and the Cross-Section of Expected Returns," is a tongue-in-cheek reference to more than 50 research papers submitted to the journal that included this line in their title, beginning with the seminal one by Fama and French (1992) that started the whole process of factor modeling.

8. A lognormal distribution has fatter tails than a normal distribution and is therefore a better match to the true distribution of stock prices, which have a fat left tail and negative skew.

9. Mandelbrot gained prominence later outside of finance for his work with fractal geometry.

10. See Lowenstein (2000), p. 236.

11. Heilbroner is author of *The Worldly Philosophers: The Lives, Times, and Ideas of the Great Economic Thinkers*, which is the second bestselling economics text of all time, just behind Samuelson's *Economics*.

12. See http://icifactbook.org/.

CHAPTER 4

1. Both norepinephrine and cortisol prepare the body for the fight-or-flight response to danger. For more on this, see Zweig (2007).

2. See also "A Survey of Behavioral Finance," by Barberis and Thaler (2002).

3. See Fox (2009), p. 298.

CHAPTER 5

1. See Dimson, Marsh, and Stauton (2014).

2. Non-U.S. long-term government bonds had an annualized real return of 1.6%, versus 4.5% for non-U.S. equities from 1900 through 2013, as per Dimson et al. (2014).

3. Available from Morningstar, Inc.

4. See Siegel (2014).

5. See Dimson et al. (2014).

6. See http://www.econ.yale.edu/~shiller/data.htm.

7. My paper "Absolute Momentum: A Simple Rule-Based Strategy and Universal Trend-Following Overlay," is included in this book as Appendix B. It includes a risk parity approach using only a 40% permanent allocation to fixed income, which is made possible due to absolute momentum.

8. Non-U.S. investors have generally had a more universal approach toward investing.

9. See Dimson et al (2014).

10. Currencies reflect relative exchange rate differences more than a buy-and-hold premium.

11. See Zaremba (2013).

12. See Inker (2010).

13. See also Li, Zhang, and Du (2011).

14. One might still consider exposure to certain commodity risk factors if one has a way to identify, isolate, and utilize them. See Blitz and De Groot (2014).

15. I use DJ-UBSCI instead of GSCI because DJ-UBSCI constrains each commodity sector to no more than one-third of the index, whereas the energy sector allocation in GSCI can be as high as 60–70%.

16. Nominal annual returns were 4.84% with a standard deviation of 10.2 and a Sharpe ratio of 0.16.

17. They developed a method to determine the false discovery rate used to adjust for data-snooping bias.

18. See Dimson et al. (2014).

19. See https://personal.vanguard.com/us/insights/investingtruths/investing-truth-about-cost.

20. See 1996 Annual Report, Chairman's Letter, Berkshire Hathaway, Inc.

21. See "A Conversation with Benjamin Graham" at http://www.bylo.org/bgraham76.html.

22. Skewness relates to the symmetrical characteristics of the return distribution. Positive skewness of returns implies greater variance of positive returns, while negative skewness implies greater variance of negative returns.

23. See Asness et al. (2013) and Moskowitz, Ooi, and Pedersen (2012).

Chapter 6

1. BlackRock (owner of iShares) and JPMorgan Chase have also switched over to the term "strategic beta."
2. Morningstar found the alpha of PRF to be negative when using a multifactor framework incorporating size, value, momentum, and quality.
3. See http://morningstar.com.
4. At the CFA Institute Annual Conference in May 2014, Nobel laureate William Sharpe remarked, "When I hear smart beta, it makes me sick. . . . I don't think it will work in the future."
5. See Haugen and Baker (1991).
6. See Chordia, Subrahmanyam, and Tong (2013), and McLean and Pontiff (2013).
7. Representative of these are Israel and Moskowitz (2013), Fama and French (2008), and Schwert (2002).
8. Warren Buffett has always favored highly profitable companies with low capital requirements, which is consistent with the factor loadings of this new Fama and French model.
9. Betas are 1.08 for momentum, 1.27 for value, and 1.26 for size. Residual volatilities are 7.60 for momentum, 11.05 for value, and 11.30 for size. Annual information ratios are 0.73 for momentum, 0.26 for value, and 0.19 for size.

Chapter 7

1. See "2014 Quantitative Analysis of Investor Behavior," Dalbar, Inc.
2. See http://www.curatedalpha.com/2011/curated-interview-with-ed-seykota-from-market-wizards/.
3. There is significant positive auto-covariance between a security's excess future return and its past excess return.
4. Lo and MacKinlay (1988) had to wait almost two years to have their paper on technical trading rules accepted, despite the soundness of their research.
5. See Brock, Lakonishok, and LeBaron (1992), Lo and MacKinlay (1999), Lo, Mamaysky, and Wang (2000), Zhu and Zhou (2009), Han, Yang, and Zhou (2011), and Han and Zhou (2013).
6. See Schwager (2012), p. 137,
7. Antonacci (2011), second place winning paper, 2011 Wagner Awards.

8. One should calculate Sharpe ratios using average monthly returns and monthly standard deviations rather than annualized figures. Some use compound annual growth rates (CAGR) instead of average returns when calculating Sharpe ratios. This double counts the effect of volatility.

9. See "Right Tail Information in Financial Markets" by Xiao (2014).

10. See Zakamouline and Koekebakker (2009) or Bacon (2013).

11. There are many other reward-to-risk measures, such as the Omega ratio, Kappa 3 ratio, and Rachev ratio. See Bacon (2013) for an extensive list.

12. Trend-following methods often tend toward positive skewness.

13. See Gray and Vogel (2013).

14. Ibid.

15. Daily drawdown would, of course, be larger.

CHAPTER 8

1. Four momentum-based products available to the public make use of 12-month momentum. AQR Capital Management LLC, QuantShares, BlackRock, and SummerHaven Index Management are the index providers for these.

2. The start date of the Barclays U.S. Aggregate Bond index is January 1, 1976. For dates prior to January 1976, we substitute the Barclays U.S. Government/Credit Bond Index, which tracks U.S. aggregate bonds closely.

3. From 1926 on, the average annual return of intermediate- and long-term bonds has been approximately the same, while the standard deviation of intermediate bonds has been 4.25 versus 7.65 for long-term bonds.

4. All indexes used are on a total return basis that includes dividend distributions.

5. There are four brokerage firms with commission-free ETFs that could be used with GEM.

6. If we leave out emerging markets by using MSCI World ex-U.S. instead of ACWI ex-U.S., average annual return is 17.0, standard deviation is 12.54, Sharpe ratio is 0.84, and maximum drawdown is –22.72.

7. Negative skewness is an indicator of left tail risk. Skewness over the entire data period is –1.05 for ACWI, –0.93 for absolute momentum, –0.54 for relative momentum, and –0.61 for GEM.

8. See http://mba.tuck.dartmouth.edu/pages/faculty/ken.french/data_library.html.

9. ETFs usually have no capital gain distributions, while mutual funds are required to pass through net capital gains when fund managers sell their holdings.

10. See http://stockcharts.com/freecharts/perf.php.

11. One can trade commission-free at Fidelity using iShares ETFs having the same 10 basis points average expense ratio, but its non-U.S. fund has less trading volume than the Vanguard fund. The average annual expense ratio of similar Schwab ETFs is only 6 basis points, but they have significantly less liquidity than the Vanguard funds.

12. Tobin came up with his separation theorem in 1958, shortly after Markowitz published his work on MVO.

CHAPTER 9

1. See http://www.forbes.com/sites/davidleinweber/2012/07/24/stupid-data-miner-tricks-quants-fooling-themselves-the-economic-indicator-in-your-pants/.

2. From talks given at Cornell in 1964 as part of the Messenger Lecture series.

3. See Cooper (2014).

4. There are now 88 years of data in the CRSP database.

5. An advantage of using the false discovery rate is its robustness with respect to cross-sectional dependencies. For more on this, see Barras et al. (2010) and Benjamini, Krieger, and Yekutieli (2006).

6. Galton discovered the concepts of standard deviation, correlation coefficient, and regression to the mean.

7. CAPE has been above 20 and overvalued for almost all of the past 20 years. For more on this subject, see http://philosophicaleconomics.wordpress.com/2014/06/08/sixpercent/.

8. See AQR Capital Management LLC, http://www.aqrindex.com.

9. This paper does a good job of debunking some common myths and misconceptions about momentum.

10. See Booth and Fama (1992) for an analysis of rebalancing profits.

CHAPTER 10

1. Someone actually interviewed Madoff in federal prison, where he is serving 150 years for securities fraud, to ask his investment recommendations: http://www.valuewalk.com/2013/06/madoff-recommends-index-funds/.

2. This applies to bonds as well as stocks. See Blake, Elton, and Gruber (1993).

3. According to Gennaioli, Shleifer, and Vishny (2012), investors pay excessive fees to active managers who underperform because trust in outside managers reduces investors' perception of investment risk.

4. For more on experts versus algorithms, see Tetlock (2005).

5. For other examples of quantitative models dominating over experts, see "Global Equity Strategy: Painting by Numbers—An Ode to Quant" by James Montier. http://www.thehedgefundjournal.com /node/7378.

6. From his 2010 MIT speech, "Mathematics, Common Sense, and Good Luck: My Life and Career," http://video.mit.edu/watch /mathematics-common-sense-and-good-luck-my-life-and-careers-9644/.

7. See http://www.traderslog.com/richard-driehaus-profile/.

8. Adapted from the traditional song "The Great Rock Island Route" by J. A. Roff (1882).

Appendix B

1. There are no transaction costs deducted for monthly rebalancing of the momentum or any benchmark portfolios.

2. Cowles and Jones (1937) were the first to point out the profitable look-back period of 12 months using U.S. stock market data from 1920 through 1935. Moskowitz et al. (2012) also found a 12-month look-back period best when applying absolute momentum to 58 liquid futures markets from 1969 through 2009.

3. For the 10 years ending December 2012, the monthly correlation of the absolute momentum 60/40 portfolio to the S&P 500 Index was 0.53, compared to a correlation of 0.87 for the normal 60/40 portfolio to the S&P 500 Index.

4. Data is from the Robert Shiller website: http://www.econ.yale .edu/~shiller/data.htm.

5. Some use covariance instead of volatility in order to take into account asset correlations.

6. DeMiguel, Garlappi, and Uppal (2009) test 14 out-of-sample allocation models on seven datasets and find that none has higher Sharpe ratios or higher certainty equivalent returns than equal weighting. Gains from optimal diversification with more complicated models are more than offset by estimation errors.

7. We use gold instead of commodities because of the possible lack of risk premia and substantial front-running rollover costs associated with commodity index futures (Daskalaki and Skiadopoulus 2011; Mou 2011).

8. Trend-following methods can also reduce negative skew and associated left tail risk (Rulle 2004). Negative skew can be especially problematic when there is leverage. Absolute momentum may reduce or eliminate negative skew.

9. Elimination of Treasury bill holdings in lieu of borrowing would reduce borrowing costs. We have not accounted for this cost saving.

10. See http://mba.tuck.dartmouth.edu/pages/faculty/ken.french/data_library.html.

GLOSSARY

T HIS GLOSSARY PROVIDES A STARTING point for better understanding the terms used in this book. I suggest doing Internet searches for more detailed information, as well as consulting the books on the Recommended Reading list.

Absolute momentum   The tendency for an asset to persist in its performance based on its own price history.

Active investment management   Portfolio strategy where a manager makes continuing investment choices with the goal of outperforming an investment benchmark.

Adjustment effect   See *Anchoring*.

Alpha   Measure of performance on a risk-adjusted basis; excess return relative to the excess return of a benchmark.

Anchoring   Relying too heavily on one piece of information and only partially updating one's views when faced with new information; slowness in accepting the full impact of information retards the price adjustment mechanism and leads to price continuation.

Animal spirits   Behavior that is motivated by emotive factors rather than by economic rationality.

Anomaly   Something that deviates from the norm, such as investment strategies that outperform expectations based on their systematic risks; situation in which performance is contrary to the idea of efficient markets.

Asymmetric loss aversion   Taking large risks in attempting to avoid loss, but risk averse in the face of potential gains; see also *Disposition effect*.

Autocorrelation   The cross-correlation of returns with themselves, also known as auto-covariance; correlation between values of a process at different times.

Backfill bias   When results are added to an index only after a few months or years of good performance; a form of self-selection bias.

Bandwagon effect   See *Herding*.

Basis points   A unit of measure in finance equal to one-hundredth of one percentage point.

Behavioral finance   Study of social, cognitive, and emotional factors on the behavior of investors and the effect this has on markets; explains why investors make irrational decisions that lead to market anomalies.

Beta   Measure of the risk arising from exposure to general market movements; risk that cannot be diversified away.

Bias   An inclination of temperament or outlook.

Bootstrap   Resampling technique to obtain estimates of sample statistics; used when the statistical distribution is complicated or unknown, or when the sample size is too small for standard statistical inferences.

Capital asset pricing model (CAPM)   Describes the relationship between risk and expected return that is used in the pricing of securities; the return on any security is proportional to the risk of that security as measured by its market beta.

Capitalization weighted   Weighting each stock by the total value of its outstanding stock; larger companies therefore account for a greater portion of a capitalization-weighted portfolio or index.

Capital market line   Straight line drawn from the point of the risk-free rate to the feasible region of risky assets.

Cognitive dissonance   Mental conflict and discomfort experienced when presented with evidence that our beliefs or assumptions are wrong.

Confirmation bias   Tendency to search for and accept information that supports our beliefs while rejecting information that contradicts them.

Conservatism   To revise one's beliefs insufficiently when presented with new evidence; tendency to find information that agrees with one's existing views while ignoring anything that contradicts them.

Correlation   Measure of the relationship between two variables indicating how things move in relation to each other; values can range from +1 (perfect correlation) to –1 (perfect negative correlation).

Cross-sectional   Comparing differences between groups at one point in time.

Curve fitting   Coincidental patterning in historical data that is unlikely to reappear going forward; see also *Overfitting bias.*

Data mining   Technique for building predictive models by discerning patterns in past data.

Data snooping   Also known as data dredging or data torturing, the inappropriate use of data mining to uncover misleading relationships; see also *Overfitting bias.*

Deciles   Splitting data into 10 equal segments.

Derivative   Financial contract that derives its value from the performance of another asset and that specifies conditions under which payments are to be made by the parties involved; includes futures, options, forwards, and swaps.

Disposition effect   Tendency to sell winners prematurely to lock in gains and to hold onto losers too long in the hope of breaking even; see also *Asymmetric loss aversion.*

Double sort   Sorting data into categories based on one factor, then sorting these categories into new categories based on an additional factor.

Drawdown   Difference between a portfolio's highest valuation and its lowest subsequent valuation; the percentage that price moves down after making a new high.

Dual momentum   A combination of absolute and relative momentum.

Efficient market hypothesis (EMH)   Idea that security prices fully reflect all publicly available information and that after adjusting for risks one cannot easily achieve long-run returns in excess of the market.

Ergodicity   Where every sequence or sizeable sample is equally representative of the whole; implies that statistical properties can be deduced from a single sample of the process.

Equal weighted   Where each stock has the same weighting or importance in a portfolio or index.

Excess return   Rate of return from a security or portfolio that exceeds the return of a benchmark or index.

Expected return   How much you can expect to earn on average on an investment.

False discovery rate   Statistical method used in hypothesis testing to account for multiple comparisons by indicating the expected percent of false predictions.

Fat-tailed   Where the probability of an extreme move is greater than the probability under a normal distribution; see also *Leptokurtosis*.

Formation period   See *Look-back period*.

Hedge funds   Pooled investment vehicles administered by professional managers and not offered to the general public, which allows them to charge higher fees and operate with greater flexibility than publically available funds.

Herding   Irrational group behavior to do or believe primarily because others do or believe the same; leads to overreaction.

Heuristic   Simple, efficient rules or mental shortcuts to explain how people make decisions under uncertainty; examples include trial and error, rule of thumb, and educated guess.

Hindsight bias   The inclination after an event has occurred to see it as having been predictable, despite having little or no objective basis for predicting it prior to its occurrence; also known as the knew-it-all-along effect.

Idiosyncratic volatility   Diversifiable risk due to the unique characteristics of a specific security; has little or no correlation with market risk.

Index fund   A passively managed investment fund that aims to replicate or track the movements of a market index; noted for relatively low operating expenses and low portfolio turnover.

Information ratio   Difference between the return of an asset or portfolio and a selected benchmark divided by the tracking error.

In sample   Data that was used to build a model or strategy.

Interquartile range   Measure of statistical dispersion equal to the difference between the first and fourth quartiles of the data.

Joint hypothesis problem   Means that market efficiency can never be fully determined on its own and any model that rejects market efficiency might itself be wrong.

Kurtosis   Describes the flatness of a distribution and the fatness of the tails; higher kurtosis implies a greater probability of extreme returns.

Leptokurtosis   Peaked mean with fat tails, indicating a high likelihood of extreme events.

Leverage   To increase the potential return and volatility of an investment; often done through borrowing.

Linear regression   An approach to model the linear relationship between a dependent variable and one or more explanatory variables; see also *Regression*.

Lognormal distribution   Continuous probability distribution of a random variable whose logarithm is normally distributed; often used for modeling financial time-series data where the variable is the multiplicative product of returns over time.

Longitudinal momentum   See *Absolute momentum*.

Look-back period   Number of prior months used for evaluating comparative past performance and determining momentum signals. See *Formation period*.

Loss aversion   Tendency to prefer avoiding losses rather than achieving gains; see also *Risk aversion*.

Market efficiency   The degree to which stock prices reflect all publically available, relevant information; see also *Efficient market hypothesis (EMH)*.

Maximum drawdown   Largest single drop from peak to valley in the value of an asset or portfolio over its entire history.

Mean reversion   Prices or returns moving back toward their average over time; regression toward the mean.

Mean-variance optimization (MVO)   Quantitative approach aimed at maximizing expected portfolio return at a given level of portfolio risk, or minimizing portfolio risk at a given level of expected return; uses past returns, correlations, and volatility.

Minimum variance portfolio   Collection of risky assets optimized to give the least amount of volatility.

Modern portfolio theory (MPT)   Theory that attempts to maximize expected portfolio return with respect to portfolio risk; a mathematical approach to optimal investment diversification.

Momentum   Persistence in performance; assets that have trended higher or lower in the recent past tend to continue trending in the same direction in the near future.

Moving average   Calculation used to create a series of averages from different data subsets then shifting each subset forward over time; commonly used to smooth out short-term fluctuations and identify longer-term trends.

Noise   Unpredictable and nonrepeatable patterns representing arbitrariness and uncertainty; noise is in contrast to information and is often mistaken as such.

Nominal return   Stated rate of return not adjusted for inflation.

Nonparametric   Having no characteristic structure; distributions whose form is unspecified.

Normal distribution   A symmetric continuous probability distribution that adheres to the familiar bell-shaped curve; has many convenient properties and is useful for drawing statistical inferences.

Out-of-sample   All new data set that is completely different from the one over which one optimizes a strategy or builds a model.

Overconfidence   Subjective belief that one's own judgment is better than it really is; the majority believe they are superior to the average; this can cause investors to underreact to new information.

Overfitting bias   When a statistical model is excessively complex and the model describes random error or noise more than an underlying relationship; characterized by poor predictive performance.

Overreaction   To react disproportionately to new information; leads to past winners being overpriced and past losers being underpriced.

Overspecification   See *Overfitting bias*.

Passive investment management   A predetermined strategy that attempts to mirror a benchmark index; also known as a buy-and-hold approach.

Private equity   Capital for investment directly into private companies not quoted on a public exchange.

Prospect theory   Explains why individuals make decisions that deviate from rational decision making by observing how they perceive expected outcomes: people value gains differently than they do losses and prefer to base decisions on perceived gains rather than perceived losses.

Quartiles   Splitting data into four equal parts.

Quintiles   Splitting data into five equal parts.

Random walk   In finance, the theory stating stock prices are independent and unpredictable; it is consistent with the efficient market hypothesis.

Rational expectations   When people make choices based on available information and experience; where expectations equal expected values and errors are random rather than systematic.

Real return   Rate of return on an investment adjusted for changes due to inflation.

Regression   An equation describing the nature of the relationship between two or more variables, including measures to assess the accuracy of that relationship.

Relative momentum   When an asset's past performance relative to that of other assets is used to predict its future performance.

Relative strength   Measure of how strong an asset's performance has been in relation to something else.

Representativeness   Subjective probability of an event determined by the degree to which it is similar to the features of its parent population; the tendency to see too many parallels between events that are not the same by inferring too quickly on the basis of too few data points.

Residual   The difference between a regression equation's fitted value and what is actually observed.

Reward-to-variability ratio   See *Sharpe ratio*.

Risk-adjusted return   Profitability adjusted to account for the risk involved in producing that return; Sharpe ratio, information ratio, and alpha are examples of risk-adjusted returns.

Risk aversion   Reluctance to accept an uncertain payoff rather than a more certain one with a lower payoff; measure of the additional reward an investor requires for accepting more risk.

Risk-free rate   Rate of return on an investment with zero risk; usually represented by the return on short-term Treasury bills.

Risk parity   Portfolio management approach where allocations are adjusted to the same volatility; often used with leverage to compensate for lower expected returns from large allocations to fixed income.

Risk premium   Return in excess of the risk-free rate that is compensation for bearing additional risk.

Robust   Continuing good performance despite changes in market conditions.

Roll yield   Return generated in rolling short-term futures contracts into longer-term ones.

Selection bias   Data selected on a nonrandom or nonuniform basis; may also apply to the selection of the data's starting date.

Self-attribution bias   The tendency to reject negative feedback and over-look our own faults and failures; to attribute successful outcomes to our own skills, often when credit is not due, and to attribute unsuccessful outcomes to bad luck.

Separation theorem   Separates the investment portfolio decision from the decision about the acceptable level of risk; the idea that there is a single optimal portfolio, then borrowing or lending, depending on one's attitude toward risk.

Serial correlation   See *Autocorrelation*.

Sharpe ratio   Excess return divided by the standard deviation of that return to determine reward per unit of risk; Sharpe ratio = (Return – Risk-free return)/Standard deviation of return.

Skewness   Measure of the symmetry of a distribution; if the left tail is more pronounced, there is negative skewness, and if the reverse is true, there is positive skewness.

Standard deviation   Measurement of dispersion about an average showing how widely returns vary over time; when the standard deviation is high, the predicted range of performance is wide, with greater volatility.

Stationary distribution   Probability distribution that does not change over time.

Stochastic   Nondeterministic or randomly determined.

Stochastic dominance   In second order stochastic dominance, risk averse investors prefer one investment over another if it has at least as high a mean return and it is more predictable.

Survivorship bias   Concentrating on things that survived and overlooking those that did not; tendency to exclude failed companies from performance studies.

Systematic risk   Risk inherent to the entire market; also known as undiversifiable risk.

Tail risk   Risk of moving more than three standard deviations from its current price.

Technical analysis   Forecasting of market action by analyzing market data itself.

Time-series momentum   See *Absolute momentum*.

Tracking error   Measure of how much a portfolio deviates from its benchmark.

Trend following   Strategy based on calculations or techniques using past prices to determine the general direction of a market.

t-Statistic   Value that allows one to determine if two data sets are significantly different from one another; used when doing hypothesis testing or computing confidence intervals.

Value investing   Strategy that attempts to buy stocks at prices that are below their intrinsic value; common measures to determine this are price-to-book and price-to-earnings ratios.

Volatility   Measure of the movement of a data series; see also *Standard deviation*.

BIBLIOGRAPHY

Ahn, Dong-Hyu, Jennifer Conrad, and Robert Dittmar (2003), "Risk Adjustment and Trading Strategies," *Review of Financial Studies* 16(2), 459–485.

Akemann, Charles A., and Werner E. Keller (1977), "Relative Strength Does Persist!" *Journal of Portfolio Management* 4(1), 38–45.

Amenc, Noël, Felix Goltz, and Véronique Le Sourd (2009), "The Performance of Characteristics-Based Indices," *European Financial Management* 15(2), 241–278.

Ang, Andrew (2012), "Mean Variance Investing," working paper.

Antonacci, Gary (2011), "Optimal Momentum: A Global Cross Asset Approach," Portfolio Management Consultants.

Antonacci, Gary (2012), "Risk Premia Harvesting Through Dual Momentum," Portfolio Management Consultants.

Antonacci, Gary (2013), "Absolute Momentum: A Universal Trend-Following Overlay," Portfolio Management Consultants.

Ariely, Dan (2009), *Predictably Irrational*, New York: HarperCollins Publishers.

Asness, Clifford S., Andrea Frazzini, Ronen Israel, and Tobias J. Moskowitz (2014), "Fact, Fiction, and Momentum Investing," working paper.

Asness, Clifford S., John Liew, and Ross Stevens (1997), "Parallels Between the Cross-Sectional Predictability of Stock and Country Returns," *Journal of Portfolio Management*, 23(3), 79–87.

Asness, Clifford S., Tobias J. Moskowitz, and Lasse J. Pedersen (2013), "Value and Momentum Everywhere," *Journal of Finance*, 68(3), 929–985.

Asness, Clifford S., R. Burt Porter, and Ross L. Stevens (2000), "Predicting Stock Returns Using Industry-Relative Firm Characteristics," working paper.

Avramov, Doron, and Tarun Chordia (2006), "Asset Pricing Models and Financial Market Anomalies," *Review of Financial Studies* 19(3), 1001–1040.

Bachelier, Louis (2006), *Louis Bachelier's Theory of Speculation: The Origins of Modern Finance*, Princeton NJ: Princeton University Press.

Bacon, Carl (2013), *Practical Risk-Adjusted Performance Measurement*, West Sussex, UK: John Wiley & Sons Ltd.

Bailey, David H., Jonathan M. Borwein, Marcos López de Prado, and Qiji Jim (2014), "Pseudo-Mathematics and Financial Charlatanism: The Effects of Backtest Overfitting on Out-of-Sample Performance," *Notices of the American Mathematical Society* 61(5), 458–474.

Bajgrowicz, Pierre, and Olivier Scaillet (2012), "Technical Trading Revisited: False Discoveries, Persistence Tests, and Transaction Costs," *Journal of Financial Economics* 106(3), 473–491.

Baker, Kent H., and Victor Ricciardi (2014), *Investor Behavior: The Psychology of Financial Planning and Investing*, Hoboken: NJ: John Wiley & Sons, Inc.

Baltas, Akindynos-Nikolaos, and Robert Kosowski (2012), "Improving Time-Series Momentum Strategies: The Role of Trading Signals and Volatility Estimators," working paper.

Bansal, Ravi, Robert F. Dittmar, and Christian T. Lundblad (2005), "Consumption, Dividends, and the Cross Section of Equity Returns," *Journal of Finance* 60(4), 1639–1672.

Barber, Brad M., and Terrance Odean (2000), "Trading Is Hazardous to Your Wealth: The Common Stock Investment Performance of Individual Investors," *Journal of Finance* 55(2), 773–806.

Barber, Brad M., and Guojun Wang (2011), "Do (Some) University Endowments Earn Alpha?" *Financial Analysts Journal* 69(5), 26–44.

Barberis, Nicholas, Andrei Shleifer, and Robert Vishny (1998), "A Model of Investor Sentiment," *Journal of Financial Economics* 49(3), 307–343.

Barberis, Nicholas, and Richard H. Thaler (2002), "A Survey of Behavioral Finance," National Bureau of Economic Research Working Paper No. 9222.

Barras, Laurent, Olivier Scaillet, and Russ Wermers (2010), "False Discoveries in Mutual Fund Performance: Measuring Luck in Estimated Alphas," *Journal of Finance* 65(1), 179–216.

Benjamini, Yoav, Abba M. Krieger, and Daniel Yekutieli (2006), "Adaptive Linear Step-Up Procedures That Control the False Discovery Rate," *Biometrika* 93(3), 491–507.

Beracha, Eli, and Hilla Skiba (2011), "Momentum in Residential Real Estate," *Journal of Real Estate Finance and Economics* 43(3), 299–320.

Bernartzi, Shlomo, and Richard H. Thaler (1995), "Myopic Loss-Aversion and the Equity Premium Puzzle," *Quarterly Journal of Economics* 110(1), 73–92.

Bhardwaj, Geetesh, Gary B. Gorton, and K. Geert Rouwenhorst (2013), "Fooling Some of the People All of the Time: The Inefficient Performance and Persistence of Commodity Trading Advisors," working paper.

Bhojraj, Sanjeev, and Bhaskaran Swaminathan (2006), "Macromomentum: Returns Predictability in International Equity Indices," *Journal of Business* 79(1), 429–451.

Bikhchandani, Sushil, David Hirshleifer, and Ivo Welch (1992), "A Theory of Fads, Fashion, Custom, and Cultural Change as Informational Cascades," *Journal of Political Economy* 100(5), 992–1026.

Blake, Christopher R., Edwin J. Elton, and Martin J. Gruber (1993), "The Performance of Bond Mutual Funds," *Journal of Business* 66(3), 370–403.

Blitz, David, and Wilma De Groot (2014), "Strategic Allocation to Commodity Factor Premiums," *Journal of Alternative Investments*, forthcoming.

Blitz, David C., and Pim Van Vliet (2008), "Global Tactical Cross-Asset Allocation: Applying Value and Momentum Across Asset Classes," *Journal of Portfolio Management* 35(1), 23–38.

Bohan, James (1981), "Relative Strength: Further Positive Evidence," *Journal of Portfolio Management* 8(1), 36–39.

Booth, David, and Eugene Fama (1992), "Diversification Returns and Asset Contributions," *Financial Analysts Journal* 48(3), 26–32.

Brock, William, Josef Lakonishok, and Blake LeBaron (1992), "Simple Technical Trading Rules and the Stochastic Properties of Stock Returns," *Journal of Finance* 47(5), 1731–1764.

Brown, David P., and Robert H, Jennings (1989), "On Technical Analysis," *Review of Financial Studies* 2(4), 527–551.

Brush, John S., and Keith E. Bowles (1983), "The Predictive Power in Relative Strength and CAPM," *Journal of Portfolio Management* 9(4), 20–23.

Busse, Jeffrey A., Amit Goyal, and Sunil Wahal (2010), "Performance and Persistence in Institutional Investment Management," *Journal of Finance* 65(2), 765–790.

Carhart, Mark M. (1997), "On Persistence in Mutual Fund Performance," *Journal of Finance* 52(1), 57–82.

Chabot, Benjamin R., Eric Ghysels, and Ravi Jagannathan (2009), "Price Momentum in Stocks: Insights from Victorian Age Data," National Bureau of Economic Research Working Paper No 14500.

Chan, Kalok, Allaudeen Hameed, and Wilson H. S. Tong (2000), "Profitability of Momentum Strategies in International Equity Markets," *Journal of Financial and Quantitative Analysis* 35(2), 153–175.

Chan, Louis K. C., Narasimhan Jegadeesh, and Josef Lokonishok (2012), "Momentum Strategies," *Journal of Finance* 51(5), 1681–1713.

Chancellor, Edward (1999), *Devil Take the Hindmost: A History of Financial Speculation*, New York: Plume Books.

Chen, Hong-Yi, Sheng-Syan Chen, Chin-Wen Hsin, and Cheng-Few Lee (2014), "Does Revenue Momentum Drive or Ride Earnings or Price Momentum?" *Journal of Banking and Finance* 38, 166–185.

Chen, Li-Wen, and Hsin-Yi Yu (2013), "Investor Attention, Visual Price Pattern, and Momentum Investing," working paper.

Chen, Long, Ohad Kadan, and Engin Kose (2009), "Fresh Momentum," working paper.

Chestnutt, George A. (1961), *Stock Market Analysis: Facts and Principles*, Larchmont, NY: American Investors Service.

Chordia, Tarun and Lakshmanan Shivakumar (2002), "Momentum, Business Cycle, and Time Varying Expected Returns," *Journal of Finance* 57(2), 985–1019.

Chordia, Tarun, Avanidhar Subrahmanyam, and Qing Tong (2013), "Trends in Capital Market Anomalies," working paper.

Chow, Tzee-man, Jason Hsu, Vitali Kalesnik, and Bryce Little (2011), "A Survey of Alternative Equity Index Strategies," *Financial Analysts Journal* 67(5), 37–57.

Conrad, Jennifer, and Gautam Kaul (1998), "An Anatomy of Trading Strategies," *Review of Financial Studies* 11(3), 489–519.

Cooper, Tony (2014), "Simulation as a Stock Market Backtesting Tool," working paper.

Covel, Michael W. (2007), *The Complete Turtle Trader: How 23 Novice Investors Became Overnight Millionaires*, New York: HarperCollins Publishers.

Cowles, Alfred III, and Herbert E. Jones (1937), "Some A Posteriori Probabilities in Stock Market Criteria," *Econometrica* 5(3), 280–294.

Daniel, Kent, David Hirshleifer, and Avanidhar Subrahmanyam (1998), "Investor Psychology and Security Market Under- and Overreactions," *Journal of Finance* 53(6), 1839–1886,

Darvas, Nicolas (1960), *How I Made $2,000,000 in the Stock Market*, Larchmont, NY: American Research Council.

Daskalaki, Charoula, and George S. Skiadopoulus (2011), "Should Investors Include Commodities in Their Portfolios After All? New Evidence," *Journal of Banking and Finance* 35(10), 2606–2626.

De Bondt, Werner F. M., and Richard Thaler (1985), "Does the Stock Market Overreact?" *Journal of Finance* 40(3), 793–805.

DeLong Bradford J., Andrei Shleifer, Lawrence H Summers, and Robert J, Waldmann (1990), "Positive Feedback Investment Strategies and Destabilizing Rational Speculation," *Journal of Finance* 45(2), 375–395.

DeMiguel, Victor, Lorenzo Garlappi, and Raman Uppal, (2009), "Optimal Versus Naïve Diversification: How Inefficient Is the 1/N Portfolio Strategy?" *Review of Financial Studies* 22(5), 1915–1953.

Dewaele, Benoit, Hughues Pirotte, Nils Tuchschmid, and Erik Wallerstein (2011), "Assessing the Performance of Funds of Hedge Funds," working paper.

Dichev, Ilia D., and Gwen Yu (2009), "Higher Risk, Lower Returns: What Hedge Funds Really Earn," *Journal of Financial Economics* 100(2), 248–263.

Dickson, Joel M., Sachin Padmawar, and Sarah Hammer (2012), "Joined at the Hip: ETF and Index Development," The Vanguard Group, Inc.

Dimson, Elroy, Paul Marsh, and Mike Staunton (2014), *Credit Suisse Global Investment Returns Yearbook 2014*, Zurich: Credit Suisse AG, 8–10.

Docherty, Paul, and Gareth Hurst (2014), "Trend Salience, Investor Behaviors, and Momentum Profitability," working paper.

Duffie, Darrell (2010), "Asset Price Dynamics with Slow-Moving Capital," *Journal of Finance* 65(4), 1238–1268.

Erb, Claude B., and Campbell R. Harvey (2006), "The Strategic and Practical Value of Commodity Futures," *Financial Analysts Journal* 62(2), 69–97.

Evans, Dylan (2012), *Risk Intelligence: How to Live with Uncertainty*, New York: Free Press.

Faber, Mebane T. (2007), "A Quantitative Approach to Tactical Asset Allocation," *Journal of Wealth Management* 9(4), 69–79.

Faber, Mebane T., and Eric W. Richardson (2009), *The Ivy Portfolio: How to Invest Like the Top Endowments and Avoid Bear Market Losses*, Hoboken, NJ: John Wiley & Sons Inc.

Fama, Eugene F. (1998), "Market Efficiency, Long-Term Returns, and Behavioral Finance," *Journal of Financial Economics* 49(3), 283–306.

Fama, Eugene, and Kenneth French (1988), "Dividend Yields and Expected Stock Returns," *Journal of Financial Economics* 22(1), 3–25.

Fama, Eugene, and Kenneth French (1992), "The Cross-Section of Expected Stock Returns," *Journal of Finance* 47(2), 427–465.

Fama, Eugene F., and Kenneth French (1993), "Common Risk Factors in the Returns on Stocks and Bonds," *Journal of Financial Economics* 33(1), 3–56.

Fama, Eugene, and Kenneth French (2004), "The Capital Asset Pricing Model: Theory and Practice," *Journal of Economic Perspective* 18(3), 25–46.

Fama, Eugene, and Kenneth French (2007), "Smart Talk: Fama and French," *Journal of Indexes* 8(4), 10–12.

Fama, Eugene, and Kenneth French (2008), "Dissecting Anomalies," *Journal of Finance* 63(4), 1653–1678.

Fama, Eugene, and Kenneth French (2010), "Luck Versus Skill in the Cross-Section of Mutual Fund Returns," *Journal of Finance* 65(5), 1915–1947.

Fama, Eugene F., and Kenneth R. French (2014), "A Five-Factor Asset Pricing Model," working paper.

Fang, Jiali, Ben Jacobsen, and Yafeng Qin (2013), "Predictability of the Simple Technical Trading Rules: An Out-of-Sample Test," *Review of Financial Economics* 23(1), 30–45.

Fang, Jiali, Yafeng Qin, and Ben Jacobsen (2014), "Technical Market Indicators: An Overview," working paper.

Feifei, Li, Vitali Kalesnik, and Jason Hsu (2012), "An Investor's Guide to Smart Beta Strategies," *AAII Journal*, American Association of Individual Investors, December 2012.

Fox, Justin (2009), *The Myth of the Rational Market*, New York: HarperCollins Publishers.

Frazzini, Andrea (2006), "The Disposition Effect and Underreaction to News," *Journal of Finance* 61(4), 2017–2046.

Friesen, Geoffrey C., Paul Weller, and Lee Dunham (2009), "Price Trends and Patterns in Technical Analysis: A Theoretical and Empirical Examination," *Journal of Banking and Finance* 33(6), 1089–1100.

Galbraith, John Kenneth (1990), *A Short History of Financial Euphoria*, New York: Penguin Books.

Gârleanu, Nicolae, and Lasse Heje Pedersen (2007), "Liquidity and Risk Management," *American Economic Review* 97(2), 193–197.

Gartley, H. M. (1935), *Profits in the Stock Market*, Pomeroy, WA: Lambert Gann Publishing.

Gartley, H. M. (1945), "Relative Velocity Statistics: Their Application in Portfolio Analysis," *Financial Analysts Journal*, 51(1), 18–20.

Geczy, Christopher, and Mikhail Samonov (2012), "212 Years of Price Momentum (The World's Longest Backtest 1801–2012)," working paper.

George, Thomas J., and Chuan-Yang Hwang (2004), "The 52-Week High and Momentum Investing," *Journal of Finance* 59(5), 2145–2176.

Gennaioli, Nicola, Andrei Shleifer, and Robert W. Vishny (2012), "Money Doctors," National Bureau of Economic Research Working Paper No. 18077.

Goetzmann, William N., and Alok Kumar (2008), "Equity Portfolio Diversification," *Review of Finance* 12(3), 433–463.

Gordon, William (1968), *The Stock Market Indicators*, Palisades Park, NJ: Investors' Press.

Gorton, Gary, and K. Geert Rouwenhorst (2006), "Facts and Fantasies about Commodity Futures," *Financial Analysts Journal* 62(2), 57–68.

Graham, Benjamin, and David L. Dodd (1951), *Security Analysis: Principles and Techniques*, New York: McGraw-Hill.

Graham, John (1999), "Herding Among Investment Newsletters: Theory and Evidence," *Journal of Finance* 54(1), 237–268.

Gray, Wesley, and Tobias Carlisle (2013), *Quantitative Value: A Practitioner's Guide to Automating Intelligent Investment and Eliminating Behavioral Errors*, Hoboken, NJ: John Wiley & Sons Inc.

Gray, Wesley, and Jack Vogel (2013), "Using Maximum Drawdown to Capture Tail Risk," working paper.

Griffin, John, Xiuqing Ji, and J. Spencer Martin (2003), "Momentum Investing and Business Credit Risk: Evidence from Pole to Pole," *Journal of Finance* 58(6), 2515–2547.

Griffin, John, Xiuqing Ji, and J. Spencer Martin (2005), "Global Momentum Strategies: A Portfolio Perspective," *Journal of Portfolio Management* 31(2), 23–39.

Griffin, John M., and Jim Xu (2009), "How Smart Are the Smart Guys? A Unique View from Hedge Fund Stock Holdings," *Review of Financial Studies* 22(7), 2531–2570.

Grinblatt, Mark, and Brian Han (2005), "Prospect Theory, Mental Accounting, and Momentum," *Journal of Financial Economics* 78(2), 311–339.

Grinblatt, Mark, Sheridan Titman, and Russ Wermers (1995), "Momentum Investment Strategies, Portfolio Performance, and Herding: A Study of Mutual Fund Behavior," *American Economic Review* 85(5), 1088–1105.

Grove, William M., David H. Zald, Boyd S. Lebow, Beth E. Snitz, and Chad Nelson (2000), "Clinical Versus Mechanical Prediction: A Meta-Analysis," *Psychological Assessment* 12(1), 19–30.

Grundy, Bruce D., and J. Spencer Martin (2001), "Understanding the Nature of the Risks and the Sources of the Rewards to Momentum Investing," *Review of Financial Studies* 14(1), 29–78.

Hader, Josef, and William R. Russell (1969), "Rules for Ordering Uncertain Prospects," *The American Economic Review* 59(1), 25–34.

Haller, Gilbert (1965), *The Haller Theory of Stock Market Trends*, West Palm Beach, FL: Gilbert Haller.

Han, Yufeng, Ke Yang, and Guofu Zhou (2011), "A New Anomaly: The Cross-Sectional Profitability of Technical Analysis," working paper.

Han, Yufeng, and Guofu Zhou (2013), "Trend Factor: A New Determinant of Cross-Section Stock Returns," working paper.

Harris, Robert S., Tim Jenkinson, and Steven N. Kaplan (2013), "Private Equity Performance: What Do We Know?" *Journal of Finance*, forthcoming.

Harvey, Campbell R., Yan Liu, and Heqing Zhu (2013), ". . . And the Cross-Section of Expected Returns," working paper.

Haugen, Robert A. (2010), *The New Finance: Overreaction, Complexity, and Uniqueness*, Upper Saddle River, NJ: Prentice Hall, Inc.

Haugen, Robert A., and Nardin L. Baker (1991), "The Efficient Market Inefficiency of Capitalization-Weighted Stock Portfolios," *Journal of Portfolio Management* 17(3), 35–40.

Higson, Chris, and Rüdiger Stucke (2012), "The Performance of Private Equity," working paper.

Hong, Harrison, and Jeremy Stein (1999), "A Unified Theory of Underreaction, Momentum Trading, and Overreaction in Asset Markets," *Journal of Finance* 54(6), 2143–2184.

Hurst, Brian, Yao Hua Ooi, and Lasse H. Pedersen (2012), "A Century of Evidence on Trend-Following Investing," AQR Capital Management, LLC.

Hurst, Brian, Yao Hua Ooi, and Lasse H. Pedersen (2014), "Demystifying Managed Futures," *Journal of Investment Management*, forthcoming.

Ilmanen, Antti (2011), *Expected Returns: An Investor's Guide to Harvesting Market Rewards*, West Sussex, UK: John Wiley & Sons Ltd.

Inker, Ben (2010), "The Hidden Risks of Risk Parity Portfolios," GMO White Paper, March 2010.

Israel, Ronen, and Tobias J. Moskowitz (2013), "The Role of Shorting, Firm Size, and Time on Market Anomalies," *Journal of Financial Economics* 108(2), 275–301.

Jacobs, Heiko, Sebastian Müller, and Martin Weber (2014), "How Should Individual Investors Diversify? An Empirical Evaluation of Alternative Asset Allocation Policies," *Journal of Financial Markets* 19, 62–85.

Jegadeesh, Narasimhan (1990), "Evidence of Predictable Behavior of Security Returns," *Journal of Finance* 45(3), 881–898.

Jegadeesh, Narasimhan, and Sheridan Titman (1993), "Returns to Buying Winners and Selling Losers: Implications for Stock Market Efficiency," *Journal of Finance* 48(1), 65–91.

Jegadeesh, Narasimhan, and Sheridan Titman (2001), "Profitability of Momentum Strategies: An Evolution of Alternative Explanations," *Journal of Finance* 56(2), 699–720.

Jensen, Michael C. (1968), "The Performance of Mutual Funds in the Period 1945–1964," *Journal of Finance* 23(2), 389–416.

Johnson, Timothy (2002), "Rational Momentum Effects," *Journal of Finance* 57(2), 585–608.

Jostova, Gergana, Stanislova Nikolova, Alexander Philipov, and Christof W Stahel (2013), "Momentum in Corporate Bond Returns," *Review of Financial Studies* 26(7), 1649–1693.

Kahneman, Daniel (2011), *Thinking, Fast and Slow*, New York: Farrar, Straus and Giroux.

Kahneman, Daniel, and Amos Tversky (1979), "Prospect Theory: An Analysis of Decision Under Risk," *Econometrica* 47(2), 263–292.

Kandasamy, Narayan, Ben Hardy, Loinel Page, Markus Schaffner, Johann Gaggaber, Andrew S. Powlson, Paul C. Fletcher, Mark Gurnell, and John Coates (2014), "Cortisol Shifts Financial Risk Preferences," *Proceedings of the National Academy of Sciences* 111(9), 3608–3613.

Keim, Donald B., and Robert F. Stambaugh (1986), "Predicting Returns in Stock and Bond Markets," *Journal of Finance* 17(2), 357–390.

Kindleberger, Charles P., and Robert Z. Aliber (2011), *Manias, Panics, and Crashes: A History of Financial Crises*, New York: Palgrave MacMillan.

King, Matthew, Oscar Silver, and Binbin Guo (2002), "Passive Momentum Asset Allocation," *Journal of Wealth Management* 5(3), 34–41.

Klein, Donald B., and Robert F. Stambaugh (1986), "Predicting Returns in Stocks and Bond Markets," *Journal of Financial Economics* 17(2), 357–390.

Knight, Timothy (2014), *Panic, Prosperity, and Progress: Five Centuries of History and the Markets*, Hoboken, NJ: John Wiley & Sons, Inc.

Kothari, S. P., Jay Shanken, and Richard G. Sloan (1995), "Another Look at the Cross-Section of Expected Returns," *Journal of Finance* 50(1), 185–224.

Kumar, Alok (2009), "Who Gambles in the Stock Market?" *Journal of Finance* 64(4), 1889–1933.

Lack, Simon A. (2012), *The Hedge Fund Mirage: The Illusion of Big Money and Why It's Too Good to Be True*, Hoboken, NJ: John Wiley & Sons Inc.

Lefèvre, Edwin (2010), *Reminiscences of a Stock Operator: With New Commentary and Insights on the Life and Times of Jesse Livermore*, Hoboken, NJ: John Wiley & Sons Inc.

Lemperiere, Y., C. Deremble, P. Seager, M. Potters, and J. P. Bouchad (2014), "Two Centuries of Trend Following," working paper.

Levy, Robert A. (1967), "Relative Strength as a Criterion for Investment Selection," *Journal of Finance* 22(4), 595–610.

Levy, Robert A. (1968), *The Relative Strength Concept of Common Stock Price Forecasting*, Larchmont, NY: Investors Intelligence, Inc.

Li, Xiaoming, Bing Zhang, and Zhijie Du (2011), "Correlation in Commodity Futures and Equity Markets Around the World: Long-Run Trend and Short-Run Fluctuation," working paper.

Liu, Laura Xiaolei, and Lu Zhang (2008), "Momentum Profits, Factor Pricing, and Macroeconomic Risk," *Review of Financial Studies* 21(6), 2417–2448.

Lo, Andrew W. (2012), "Why Buy and Hold Doesn't Work Anymore," *Money* magazine, March issue.

Lo, Andrew W., and A. Craig MacKinlay (1988), "Stock Market Prices Do Not Follow Random Walks: Evidence from a Simple Specification Test," *The Review of Financial Studies* 1(1), 41–66.

Lo, Andrew W., and A. Craig MacKinlay (1999), *A Non-Random Walk Down Wall Street*, Princeton: NJ, Princeton University Press.

Lo, Andrew W., Harry Mamaysky, and Jiang Wang (2000), "Foundations of Technical Analysis: Computational Algorithms, Statistical Inference, and Empirical Implementation," *Journal of Finance* 55(4), 1705–1770.

Lombardi, Marco J., and Francesco Ravazzolo (2013), "On the Correlation Between Commodity and Equity Returns: Implications for Portfolio Allocation," Bank for International Settlements Working Paper No. 420.

López de Prado, Marcos (2013), "What to Look for in a Backtest," Hass Energy Trading Corp.

Lowenstein, Roger (2000), *When Genius Failed: The Rise and Fall of Long-Term Capital Management*, New York: Random House.

MacKenzie, Donald (2006), *An Engine, Not a Camera: How Financial Models Shape Markets*, Cambridge, MA: MIT Press.

Malkiel, Burton G. (1995), "Returns from Investing in Equity Mutual Funds," *Journal of Finance* 50(2), 549–572.

Mandelbrot, Benoit, and Richard L Hudson (2004), *The Misbehavior of Markets: A Fractal View of Financial Turbulence*, New York: Basic Books.

Marshall, Ben R., Rochester H. Cahan, Jared M. Cahan (2008), "Can Commodity Futures Be Profitably Traded with Quantitative Market Timing Strategies?" *Journal of Banking and Finance* 32(9), 1810–1819.

McLean, R. David, and Jeffrey Pontiff (2013), "Does Academic Research Destroy Stock Return Predictability?" working paper.

Menkoff, Lukas, Lucio Sarno, Maik Schmeling, and Andreas Schrimpf (2011), "Currency Momentum Strategies," working paper.

Meub, Lukas, and Till Proeger (2014), "An Experimental Study on Social Anchoring," working paper.

Meucci, Attilo (2009), *Risk and Asset Allocation*, New York: Springer Finance.

Miffre, Joelle, and Georgios Rallis (2007), "Momentum Strategies in Commodity Futures Markets," *Journal of Banking and Finance* 31(6), 1863–1886.

Mitchell, Mark, Lasse Heje Pedersen, and Todd Pulvino (2007), "Slow Moving Capital," *American Economic Review* 97(2), 215–220.

Moskowitz, Tobias J., and Mark Grinblatt (1999), "Do Industries Explain Momentum?" *Journal of Finance* 54(4), 1249–1290.

Moskowitz, Tobias J., Yao Hua Ooi, and Lasse Heje Pedersen (2012), "Time Series Momentum," *Journal of Financial Economics* 104(2), 228–250.

Mou, Yiqun (2011), "Limits to Arbitrage and Commodity Index Investment: Front-Running the Goldman Yield," working paper.

Mouboussin, Michael J. (2008), *More Than You Know: Finding Financial Wisdom in Unconventional Places*, New York: Columbia University Press.

Newey, Whitney K., and Kenneth D. West (1987), "A Simple, Positive Semi-Definite, Heteroskedasticity and Autocorrelation Consistent Covariance Matrix," *Econometrica* 55(3), 703–708.

Nofsinger, John R. (2013), *Psychology of Investing*, 5th ed., Upper Saddle River, NJ: Prentice Hall.

Odean, Terrance (1998), "Are Investors Reluctant to Realize Their Losses?" *Journal of Finance* 53(5), 1775–1798.

Okunev, John, and Derek White (2000), "Do Momentum Based Strategies Still Work in Foreign Currency Markets?" *Journal of Financial and Quantitative Markets* 38(2), 425–447.

O'Neil, William J. (2009), *How to Make Money in Stocks: A Winning System in Good Times and Bad Times*, New York: McGraw-Hill.

Park, Cheol-Ho, and Scott H. Irwin (2007), "What Do We Know About the Profitability of Technical Analysis?" *Journal of Economic Surveys* 21(4), 786–826.

Pastor, Lubos, and Robert F. Stambaugh (2003), "Liquidity Risk and Expected Stock Returns," *Journal of Political Economy* 111(3), 642–685.

Perold, André (2007), "Perspectives: Fundamentally Flawed Indexing," *Financial Analysts Journal* 63(6), 31–37.

Pirrong, Craig (2005), "Momentum in Futures Markets," working paper.

Rapach, David, Jack K. Strauss, and Guofu Zhou (2013), "International Stock Market Return Predictability: What Is the Role of the United States?" *Journal of Finance* 68(4).

Rhea, Robert (1932), *The Dow Theory*, New York: Barron's.

Ricciardi, Victor, and Helen K. Simon (2000), "What Is Behavioral Finance?" *Business, Education, and Technology Journal* 2(2), 1–9.

Rouwenhorst, K. Geert (1998), "International Momentum Strategies," *Journal of Finance* 53(1), 267–284.

Rouwenhorst, K. Geert (1999), "Local Return Factors and Turnover in Emerging Stock Markets," *Journal of Finance* 54(4), 1439–1464.

Sagi, Jacob, and Mark Seasholes (2007), "Firm-Specific Attributes and the Cross-Section of Momentum," *Journal of Financial Economics* 84(2), 389–434.

Samuelson, Paul A. (1974), "Challenge to Judgment," *Journal of Portfolio Management* 1(1), 17–19.

Schwager, Jack D. (2008), *The New Market Wizards: Conversations with America's Top Traders*, Hoboken, NJ: John Wiley & Sons Inc.

Schwager, Jack D. (2012), *Market Wizards: Interviews with Top Traders*, Hoboken, NJ: John Wiley & Sons Inc.

Schwert, G. William (2002), "Anomalies and Market Efficiency," National Bureau of Economic Research Working Paper No. 9277.

Seamans, George (1939), *The Seven Pillars of Stock Market Success*, Brightwaters, NY: Windsor Books.

Sewell, Martin (2011), *History of the Efficient Market Hypothesis*, UCL Department of Computer Science.

Sharpe, William F. (1994), "The Sharpe Ratio," *Journal of Portfolio Management* 21(10), 49–58.

Shefrin, Hersh, and Meir Statman (1985), "The Disposition to Sell Winners Too Early and Ride Losers Too Long: Theory and Evidence," *Journal of Finance* 40(3), 777–790.

Shiller, Robert J. (1981), "Do Stock Prices Move Too Much to Be Justified by Subsequent Changes in Dividends?" *American Economic Review* 71(3), 421–436.

Shiller, Robert J. (1992), *Market Volatility*, Cambridge, MA: MIT Press.

Shiller, Robert J. (2003), "From Efficient Markets Theory to Behavioral Finance," *Journal of Economic Perspectives* 17(1), 83–100.

Shiller, Robert J. (2006), *Irrational Exuberance*, 2d ed., New York: Crown Books.

Shleifer, Andrei (2000), *Inefficient Markets: An Introduction to Behavioral Finance*, New York: Oxford University Press.

Shumway, Tyler, and Vincent A. Warther (1999), "The Delisting Bias in CRSP's NASDAQ Data and Its implications for Interpretation of the Size Effect," *Journal of Finance* 54(6), 2361–2379.

Siegel, Jeremy (2014), *Stocks for the Long Run: The Definitive Guide to Financial Market Returns and Long-Term Investment Strategies*, New York: McGraw-Hill.

Soros, George (2003), *The Alchemy of Finance*, Hoboken, NJ: John Wiley & Sons, Inc.

Tang, Ke, and Wei Xiong (2012), "Index Investment and Financialization of Commodities," *Financial Analysts Journal* 68(6), 54–74.

Tanous, Peter J. (1999), *Investment Gurus: A Road Map to Wealth from the World's Best Investment Managers*, New York: Prentice Hall Direct.

Tetlock, Philip E. (2005), *Expert Political Judgment: How Good Is It? How Can We Know?*, Princeton, NJ: Princeton University Press.

Thaler, Richard T. (1994), *The Winner's Curse: Paradoxes and Anomalies of Economic Life*, Princeton NJ: Princeton University Press.

Thorp, Edward O., and Sheen T. Kassouf (1967), *Beat the Market: A Scientific Stock Market System*, New York: Random House.

Tversky, Amos, and Daniel Kahneman (1974), "Judgment Under Uncertainty: Heuristics and Biases," *Science* 185, 1124–1131.

Wason, P. C. (1960), "On the Failure to Eliminate Hypotheses in a Conceptual Task," *Quarterly Journal of Experimental Psychology* 12(3), 129–140.

Weatherall, James Owen (2013), *The Physics of Wall Street: A Brief History of Predicting the Unpredictable*, New York: Houghton Mifflin Harcourt Publishing.

Weber, Joachim, Steffen Meyer, Benjamin Loas, and Andreas Hackenthal (2014), "Which Investment Behaviors Really Matter for Individual Investors?" working paper.

Welch, Ivo (2000), "Herding Among Security Analysts," *Journal of Financial Economics* 58(3), 369–396.

West, John, and Ryan Larson (2014), "Slugging It Out in the Equity Arena," *Fundamentals*, April issue, Research Affiliates, LLC.

Wyckoff, Richard D. (1924), *How I Trade in Stocks and Bonds: Being Some Methods Evolved and Adapted During My Thirty-Three Years' Experience in Wall Street*, New York: Magazine of Wall Street.

Xiao, Zhijie (2014), "Right Tail Information in Financial Markets," *Econometric Theory* 30(1), 94–126.

Zakamouline, Valeri, and Steen Koekebakker (2009), "Portfolio Performance Evaluation with Generalized Sharpe Ratios: Beyond the Mean and Variance," *Journal of Banking and Finance* 33(7), 1242–1254.

Zaremba, Adam (2013), "Implications of Financialization for Commodity Investors: The Case of Roll Yields," working paper.

Zhou, Guofu, and Yingzi Zhu (2014), "A Theory of Technical Trading Using Moving Averages," working paper.

Zhu, Yingzi, and Guofu Zhou (2009), "Technical Analysis: An Asset Allocation Perspective on the Use of Moving Averages," *Journal of Financial Economics* 92(3), 519–544.

Zweig, Jason (2007), *Your Money and Your Brain: How the New Science of Neuroeconomics Can Help Make You Rich*, New York: Simon & Schuster.

RECOMMENDED READING

Know thyself.

—Socrates

THOSE WANTING MORE IN-DEPTH INFORMATION about relative and absolute momentum should consult the research papers listed in the bibliography. You should be able to find most of them online by doing a search on their titles or the authors' names. Many are also available on the Social Science Research Network (SSRN):

http://papers.ssrn.com/sol3/DisplayAbstractSearch.cfm.

As we know from George Santayana, those who cannot learn from history are doomed to repeat it. In the words of Warren Buffett's mentor, Benjamin Graham, "The investor's chief problem and even his worst enemy is likely to be himself." The following books deal primarily with investor psychology, behavioral finance, and the history of financial markets. They should help you make better investment decisions.

Ariely, Dan (2009), *Predictably Irrational*, New York: HarperCollins Publishers.
Baker, Kent H., and Victor Ricciardi (2014), *Investor Behavior: The Psychology of Financial Planning and Investing*, Hoboken: NJ: John Wiley & Sons, Inc.
Chancellor, Edward (1999), *Devil Take the Hindmost: A History of Financial Speculation*, New York: Plume Books.
Galbraith, John Kenneth (1990), *A Short History of Financial Euphoria*, New York: Penguin Books.
Evans, Dylan (2012), *Risk Intelligence: How to Live with Uncertainty*, New York: Free Press.

Fox, Justin (2009), *The Myth of the Rational Market*, New York: HarperCollins Publishers.

Ilmanen, Antti (2011), *Expected Returns: An Investor's Guide to Harvesting Market Rewards*, West Sussex, UK: John Wiley & Sons Ltd.

Kahneman, Daniel (2011), *Thinking, Fast and Slow*, New York: Farrar, Straus and Giroux.

Kindleberger, Charles P., and Robert Z. Aliber (2011), *Manias, Panics, and Crashes: A History of Financial Crises*, New York: Palgrave MacMillan.

Knight, Timothy (2014), *Panic, Prosperity, and Progress: Five Centuries of History and the Markets*, Hoboken, NJ: John Wiley & Sons, Inc.

Mauboussin, Michael J. (2008), *More Than You Know: Finding Financial Wisdom in Unconventional Places*, New York: Columbia University Press.

Nofsinger, John R. (2013), *The Psychology of Investing*, 5th ed., Upper Saddle River, NJ: Prentice Hall.

Shiller, Robert J. (2006), *Irrational Exuberance*, 2d ed., New York: Crown Books.

Shleifer, Andrei (2001), *Inefficient Markets: An Introduction to Behavioral Finance*, New York: Oxford University Press.

Thaler, Richard T. (1994), *The Winner's Curse: Paradoxes and Anomalies of Economic Life*, Princeton, NJ: Princeton University Press.

Weatherall, James Owen (2013), *The Physics of Wall Street: A Brief History of Predicting the Unpredictable*, New York: Houghton Mifflin Harcourt Publishing.

INDEX

ABOUT THE AUTHOR

Gary Antonacci has over 35 years' experience as an investment professional focusing on underexploited investment opportunities. His innovative research on momentum investing was the first-place winner in 2012 and the second-place winner in 2011 of the prestigious Wagner Awards for Advance in Active Investment Management given annually by the National Association of Active Investment Managers (NAAIM).

Antonacci is developer of the dual momentum–based Global Equities Momentum, Global Balanced Momentum, and Sector Rotation Momentum models. His research introduced the investment world to dual momentum, which combines relative strength price momentum with trend-following absolute momentum. He is widely recognized as a foremost authority on the practical applications of momentum investing.

Antonacci received his MBA degree from the Harvard Business School in 1978. Since then, he has concentrated on researching, developing, and applying innovative investment strategies that have their basis in academic research. He serves as a consultant on asset allocation, portfolio construction, and advanced momentum strategies.

Antonacci was at one time a U.S. Army combat medic in Vietnam and an award-winning artist. He has been active for years with dog rescue and foster care. One can find out more about Gary Antonacci and his work at http://optimalmomentum.com.